The Prophetic Mantle
&
The Reformation of the
Prophetic Ministry

Apostle Daniel L. Akins

Creative Touch Publishing LLC.

Creative Touch Publishing

Published by Creative Touch Publishing LLC.
P.O. Box 7482
Warner Robins, GA 31095
ctpublishing14@gmail.com

Printed and bound in the United States of America

International Standard Book Number
978-0-578-70499-9

❧ TABLE OF CONTENTS ❧

Dedication. 4

Acknowledgements. 5

Foreword. 6

Introduction. 7

Chapter 1: The Prophetic Mantle. 9

Chapter 2: The Gift of Prophecy. 23

Chapter 3: The Office of the Prophet/Prophetess. . . .45

Chapter 4: Growing Prophets. 55

Chapter 5: Prophetic Fathering/Mentorship. 65

Chapter 6: Prophetic Purity. 81

Chapter 7: Ministering to the Lord. 101

Chapter 8: Prophets Must Learn How to Keep
A Poor Spirit. 113

Chapter 9: Prophetic Protocol. 127

❧ DEDICATION ❧

I dedicate this book to one who is dear to our hearts, my oldest spiritual daughter, Elder Angela Fleming. She has been with our ministry for nearly twenty years. That, in itself, is almost unheard of in the times we live in. Elder Angela has proven to be faithful and unwavering in her service and commitment to God and to our ministry. She became our Administrative Elder about 4 years ago, and as my wife and I transitioned to Texas, we left the ministry in her hands to help oversee it.

Elder Angela, you have made that which we've had to do easy. You are a modern-day Phoebe and Junia, both to our lives and to our ministry (Romans 16:1-2). Your faith and obedience have caused the work of the Lord to continue without interruption. Every church and pastor needs an Elder Angela, one who is self-sacrificing, hard-working, submitted, and a genuinely loving person.

Elder Angela Fleming, I dedicate this book to you. Thank you for all that you do.

Sincerely,
Your Father in the Lord,
Apostle Daniel L. Akins

❧ ACKNOWLEDGEMENTS ❧

With much gratefulness and appreciation, I want to thank my wife of twenty-three years, Vonyett Akins. You have been here from the beginning; winning and losing with me. Throughout it all you have remained the same. Love you much!

To my Voice of Many Waters Apostolic Alliance of Churches: The pastors in this fellowship have been amazing and so supportive of my wife and I. You all have made me better in so many ways. May God continue to bless you all.

To Prophetess Thedoshia Shealey and Creative Touch Publishing LLC. Thank you for capturing my heart and tapping into the river of this prophetic flow as I've tried to scribe my thoughts. You are graced to do what you do so effortlessly. Your creative touch is evident on these pages. Many blessings upon you!

✌ FOREWORD ✍

The anointing that I have witnessed on the life of Daniel Akins is pure. I began observing this young man in 1998 when I started my first Pastorate in Milford, DE. He and another young man always attended our Friday night services. Sitting in the back of the church, he would feast on the Word and soak in the anointing of God. I watched him grow into a Prophet of God, very deliberate and blessed with a mantle of God on his life. Throughout the years, I have followed him in ministry. He has always had a desire for souls and for righteousness.

I recall him starting a storefront church in Seaford, DE then moving to Georgia, where he started another ministry. I believe his greatest passion was operating in the prophetic; it is probably one of his greatest gifts. He often traveled, hosting revivals in Florida, Delaware, Maryland, Texas, New York, and other locations. He went wherever God needed him to go.

I thank God for raising this vessel up to be a voice in these times of uncertainty.

With My Blessing,
Apostle Isaac Ross
Lead Pastor: Miracle Revival Center in Seaford, DE

❧ INTRODUCTION ❧

The Prophetic Mantle and the Reformation of the Prophetic Ministry, explains the various realms of prophetic ministry and the reformation that is so desperately needed. Practical protocol, rules, and guidelines that are essential for prophetic ministers to operate effectively and in the order of God is provided. This book is carefully designed and written for both beginners and well-seasoned prophetic ministers. It is filled with apostolic reformation and explains the basic elements of prophetic ministry.

Those who are well-versed in prophetic ministry will be stirred and challenged to take a deeper look at the scriptures, as a fresh perspective is provided throughout this book. Apostolic admonishing is given to those who have avoided proper training and fatherly instruction in the prophetic.

God is restructuring and reshaping the prophetic ministry by laying an ax to the root of our prophetic practices. As we, the Body of Christ, adopt and exercise the patterns laid out by God, we will realign ourselves to walk orderly and we will see honor restored back to the prophetic ministry.

❧ CHAPTER ONE ❧

"The Prophetic Mantle"

There are three primary realms of the prophetic dimension; four if you include the Word of God which is a more sure word of prophecy (2 Peter 1:19). In the first three chapters of this book we will discuss those three realms in brevity.

The first realm of prophecy is the spirit of prophecy.

"And I fell at his feet to worship him. And he said unto me, See thou do it not: I am thy fellow servant, and of thy brethren that have the testimony of Jesus: worship God: for the testimony of Jesus is the spirit of prophecy."

Revelation 19:10 (KJV)

John had a vision which was made known to him by an angel, and as he became overwhelmed in the moment, he began to worship the angel who carried the message rather than the one who sent the message. Let us never be tempted to worship the creature above the creator (Romans 1:25). Angels are created beings just as we are; they are not objects of worship (Colossians 2:18).

The angel quickly informed John, saying, "I'm your fellow servant and of thy brethren that have the testimony of Jesus: worship God: for the testimony of Jesus is the spirit of prophecy." The spirit of prophecy is the martyria; testimony, attestation, or evidence of Jesus.

The phrase testimony can be understood both subjectively and objectively. If Jesus is the subject, then He is the source of the testimony; it came from Him. If He is the object, then it is about Him and concerns Him. This verse teaches that the spirit of prophecy is the testimony from Jesus and about Jesus (the Word of God).

The spirit of prophecy is a realm that all believers can operate in with faith and yielding. The more Word you have in you, the easier it is to flow in this realm because it's the testimony of Jesus. In this realm, the spirit of prophecy flows through a believer unctioning them to release bits and pieces of scripture by way of rhema.

Let's look at a few examples of this in the scriptures. Take a moment to read the following scriptures: **Revelation 1:9; Revelation 6:9; Psalm 40:7; Hebrews 10:7; Luke 24:25; and John 5:39**.

"**39 And Mary arose in those days, and went into the hill country with haste, into a city of Juda; 40 And entered into the house of Zacharias, and saluted Elisabeth. 41 And it came to pass, that, when Elisabeth heard the salutation of Mary, the babe leaped in her womb; and Elisabeth was filled with the Holy Ghost: 42 And she spake out with a loud voice, and said, Blessed art thou among women, and blessed is the fruit of thy womb.**"

Luke 1:39-42 KJV)

In this passage of scripture, we see both the testimony of Jesus and the spirit of prophecy at work. It had been prophesied way back in Genesis that the Messiah would come through a woman (Genesis 3:14-15). Through the spirit of prophecy, Isaiah also gave prophetic insight of the birth of Jesus years before it happened (Isaiah 9:6).

In Luke 1:26-35 the angel Gabriel was sent from God to Mary, the mother of Jesus, to announce to her that she had found favor with God and that she would conceive a child without the help of a man, or in the natural order of child conception. In verse 35, the angel told her that the child would be conceived by the Holy Ghost; who is the author of prophecy.

Prophecy is only possible by the Spirit of God (1 Peter 1:10-12; 2 Peter 1:19-21). Through Jesus' conception, we see that His testimony is the spirit of prophecy; He came in the volume of the book.

Elisabeth heard the salutation of Mary and the Bible says, "the babe leaped for joy in her womb. She spake with a LOUD VOICE and began to prophesy to Mary." It wasn't a deep word of prophecy, nevertheless it was a Word from the Lord. Elisabeth confirmed Mary in regards to the way God was dealing with her through the spirit of prophecy. "Blessed art thou among women, and blessed is the fruit of thy womb" (Luke 1:42).

I've known people to belittle the spirit of prophecy because they didn't have an understanding of how it works. I recall one individual saying, "I don't need God to tell me He loves me. I already know that." An individual flowing in the spirit of prophecy might give the same word under the influence of the Holy Spirit, however, it may be given with more weight, comfort, edification, and exhortation attached to it. Why? Because now, the life of the Spirit is communicating it. Jesus said, "the words that I speak, they are spirit and life" (John 6:63).

Once Mary heard Elisabeth's words, the spirit of prophecy jumped on her, and she began singing prophetically (Luke 1:46-56). We are told to, "Let the message of Christ dwell among you richly as you teach and admonish one another with all wisdom through psalms, hymns, and songs from the Spirit, singing to God with gratitude in your hearts" (Colossians 3:16 NIV).

"[57] Now Elisabeth's full time came that she should be delivered; and she brought forth a son. [58] And her neighbours and her cousins heard how the Lord had shewed great mercy upon her; and they rejoiced with her. [59] And it came to pass, that on the eighth day they came to circumcise the child;

and they called him Zacharias, after the name of his father. 60 And his mother answered and said, Not so; but he shall be called John. 61 And they said unto her, There is none of thy kindred that is called by this name." 62 And they made signs to his father, how he would have him called. 63 And he asked for a writing table, and wrote, saying, His name is John. And they marvelled all. 64 And his mouth was opened immediately, and his tongue loosed, and he spake, and praised God. 65 And fear came on all that dwelt round about them: and all these sayings were noised abroad throughout all the hill country of Judaea. 66 And all they that heard them laid them up in their hearts, saying, What manner of child shall this be! And the hand of the Lord was with him. 67 And his father Zacharias was filled with the Holy Ghost, and prophesied, saying. . ."

Luke 1:57-67 (KJV)

Here is another example of the spirit of prophecy in operation concerning the testimony of Jesus Christ. Elisabeth's full time had come to give birth to John the Baptist; the forerunner of Jesus Christ. On the eight day, when it was time to circumcise the child, they called him Zacharias, but his mother answered and said, "Not so, but he shall be called John."

When God is doing something new, He normally interrupts our traditions and the things we are familiar with. Too many churches/believers have stopped walking with God because they didn't have the alacrity to move with the cloud of His leading. They have fallen in love with what God did and not with what He is doing. They are ever clutching to the jawbone of an ass after it's run its course. The Bible says once Sampson killed a thousand Philistines with the jawbone, he threw it down (Judges 15:15-17). I believe this is somebody's prophetic word! Let me get back on task.

Elisabeth's family and friends didn't understand the new thing. They said, "nobody in your family is called by this name." Sometimes those closest to us make it hard for us to embrace the new thing God is doing. Perhaps that is why Jacob was left alone with the angel (Genesis 32:24).

They made signs to Zacharias of what he would have him called. He asked for a writing table and wrote, saying, his name is John.

During that time, Zachariah's mouth was muted because initially, he didn't believe the angel's word (Luke 1:18-20). However, as soon as he agreed with God, the Bible says, "his mouth was opened immediately, and his tongue was loosed, and he spake, and praised God" (Luke 1:64). The Bible also says, "at that moment Zacharias was filled with the Holy Ghost, and prophesied, **SAYING"** (Luke 1:68). The spirit of prophecy fell on him and he began releasing the Word of the Lord concerning Old Testament scriptures relating to Jesus and John the Baptist. Although these things had already been prophesied and written; the difference was that the Holy Spirit was inspiring his words as he revealed rhema (bits and pieces of logos).

How to Flow In the Spirit of Prophecy

Worship is a vital key to flowing in the spirit of prophecy.

"And I fell at his feet to worship him. And he said unto me, See thou do it not: I am thy fellow servant, and of thy brethren that have the testimony of Jesus: worship God: for the testimony of Jesus is the spirit of prophecy."

Revelation 19:10 (KJV)

Worship and prophetic ministry join hand in hand. When we worship God, it stirs a strong prophetic presence to prophesy, but worship alone does not guarantee a prophetic flow, especially if faith and yielding are not present. I have visited churches that had dynamic singers and worship leaders, but when the spirit of prophecy came in, there was no release of it because the people had not been taught about it. As a result, Jesus wasn't released to speak prophetically to His church by song or voice. Jesus passed them by because no one apprehended him **(Mark 6:48).**

Every real worshipper is prophetic. Some just don't know it. I tell people all the time, "if you are a worshipper and you are filled with the Spirit of God you have already flowed in the spirit of prophecy at some point." Many have done it with a prayer partner or while ministering to friends or family, but most didn't know it.

When I came home from prison years ago, I was reading and fasting uncommonly. I would go out and evangelize, sharing my faith and testifying of what Jesus had done for me. In the process of doing so, I would feel unusual unctions which I didn't understand at the time. Certain scriptures and words would spring out of me before I knew it. At the time, I didn't fully understand, but I could recognize it was divinely inspired.

Later, as I had been taught in the prophetic, I realized I was flowing in the spirit of prophecy. My time of worshipping God in secret was being rewarded openly. The more you worship God, it opens you up and spiritual songs are activated. That is, songs birthed by the Spirit of God (Ephesians 5:19-20; Colossians 3:16-17).

When a church is open to prophetic worship it invites Jesus to speak His counsel to the church by song or voice. The result is an edified and strengthened church.

"I will incline mine ear to a parable: I will open my dark saying upon the harp."

Psalm 49:4 (KJV)

"⁵ After that thou shalt come to the hill of God, where is the garrison of the Philistines: and it shall come to pass, when thou art come thither to the city, that thou shalt meet a company of prophets coming down from the high place with a psaltery, and a tabret, and a pipe, and a harp, before them; and they shall prophesy: ⁶ And the Spirit of the LORD will come upon thee, and thou shalt prophesy with them, and shalt be turned into another man."

1 Samuel 10:5-6 (KJV)

David understood the power and connection between worship and the prophetic. He understood that worship was a key component to opening the heavens and to accessing the mysteries of God. There are times when I stand in my pulpit with absolutely nothing to preach; after having studied all week. Sometimes I don't feel comfortable enough to release it, but the moment I begin to worship prophetically, my heart is opened and the mysteries of scripture opens in ways unbeknown to me.

David said, "upon the harp, dark sayings were opened." David was a prophet; he introduced prophetic worship to the nation of Israel. Many of his psalms were birthed upon his harp. Worship and the spirit of prophecy ushered Saul into King Saul. Samuel gave Saul a prophetic word that he would meet a company of prophets coming down from the high place with instruments of worship before them. He went on to say that they would prophesy.

You see, in those days the prophets associated with those who could play instruments. They used worship to heighten their spiritual senses to flow prophetically. We also see this with Elisha, when he called for a minstrel in 2 Kings 3:15-16.

When Saul had the encounter with the prophets, they prophesied by the spirit of prophecy. The Bible says, Samuel told him that the Spirit would come upon him and he would prophesy, "with them." When the flow of worship is strong, we can all tap into the spirit of prophecy. The Bible says, "ye may all prophesy" (1 Corinthians 14:31).

Faith Element

"Having then gifts differing according to the grace that is given to us, whether prophecy, let us prophesy according to the proportion of faith;"

Romans 12:6 (KJV)

Faith is needed to move in the spirit of prophecy. The kingdom of God operates by the law of love and faith (Galatians 5:6). "For without faith it is impossible to please God" (Hebrews 11:6). Prophecy is not just foretelling, it is forth-telling too. It is revealing what God is saying at any given moment as His heart is expressed. It's not always something in the future or predictive.

The more faith you have that God is speaking through you the greater your prophetic flow will be. Years ago, I recall visiting local churches where the spirit of worship was strong. The spirit of prophecy would be present and for a moment, silence would come over the sanctuary. In that moment, I would feel a bubbling and impressions upon heart to release the Word of the Lord. Initially, fear would grab me prohibiting me from releasing, but to increase my faith and let me know it was Him speaking to me, God would allow someone to release what He had placed on my heart to release. This reassured me that God was speaking to me.

After this happened a few times, I immediately began responding in faith. At the time, I had no training in prophetic ministry, as it relates to flowing in a local corporate setting, but as my faith to prophesy grew, I prophesied longer and with more confidence. Initially, my faith only allowed me to say a few things, but as my faith and my Word level increased, so did my prophetic utterances. Over time, the prophetic words I released became longer and had more substance to them.

I've witnessed people who have come to our School of the Prophets, and who were initially timid, grow into some strong prophetic ministers and prophets. They got into a safe and rich environment that allowed them to develop and grow prophetically.

❧ CHAPTER TWO ❧

"The Gift of Prophecy"

The second realm of prophecy is the gift of prophecy.

"¹Follow after charity and desire spiritual gifts, but rather that ye may prophesy. ² For he that speaketh in an unknown tongue speaketh not unto men, but unto God: for no man understandeth him; howbeit in the spirit he speaketh mysteries. ³ But he that prophesieth speaketh unto men to edification, and exhortation, and comfort."

1 Corinthians 14:1-3 (KJV)

"Now concerning spiritual gifts, brethren, I would not have you ignorant."

1 Corinthians 12:1 (KJV)

"⁷ But the manifestation of the Spirit is given to every man to profit withal. ⁸ For to one is given by the Spirit the word of wisdom; to another the word of knowledge by the same Spirit; ⁹ To another faith by the same Spirit; to another the

gifts of healing by the same Spirit; [10] To another the working of miracles; to another prophecy; to another discerning of spirits; to another divers kinds of tongues; to another the interpretation of tongues:"

1 Corinthians 12:7-10 (KJV)

The gift of prophecy is one of the nine gifts of the Spirit we read about in 1 Corinthians 12:7-11. The gifts of the Spirit, according to the Bible, are to be desired. The word desire here means: "to be jealous of" or "to lust after" (1 Corinthians 14:1).

One of the greatest hindrances to moving in the gifts of the Spirit is not desiring them. I have encountered many people throughout the years who have religiously spoken against operating in the gifts of the Spirit; as though it is a sin to want gifts.

Gifts, like guns are not a problem. Both only become an issue when placed in the wrong hands. We are instructed to desire spiritual gifts. The church cannot be as strong as it needs to be without the gifts of the

Spirit in operation. Gifts edify the church and assist in destroying the works of the devil (1 John 3:8).

I find it interesting that out of all the gifts to be desired, Paul said, "but rather that ye may prophesy." It is obvious that Paul understood how important prophecy was. God gives us a glimpse of His heart concerning prophetic ministry through the taking of Moses' spirit and placing it on seventy of his elders.

"24 And Moses went out, and told the people the words of the LORD, and gathered the seventy men of the elders of the people, and set them round about the tabernacle. 25 And the LORD came down in a cloud, and spake unto him, and took of the spirit THAT WAS UPON HIM, AND GAVE IT TO THE SEVENTY ELDERS: and it came to pass, that, when the spirit rested upon them, they PROPHESIED, and did not cease. 26 But there remained two of the men in the camp, the name of the one was Eldad, and the name of the other Medad: and the spirit rested upon them; and they were of them that were written, but went not out unto the tabernacle: and they prophesied in the camp. 27 And there ran a young man, and told Moses, and

said, Eldad and Medad do prophesy in the camp.
^{28} And Joshua the son of Nun, the servant of Moses,
one of his young men, answered and said, My lord
Moses, forbid them. ^{29} And Moses said unto him,
Enviest thou for my sake? would God that ALL THE
LORD'S PEOPLE WERE PROPHETS, AND THAT THE
LORD WOULD PUT HIS SPIRIT UPON THEM!"

Numbers 11:24-29 (KJV)

This passage of scripture gives us a little insight into
the heart of God concerning prophetic ministry and
the spirit of prophecy. The scriptures ask, "Are all
apostles? Are all prophets? Are all teachers? Are all
workers of miracles?" (1 Corinthians 12:29). The
answer is no!

The previous scripture tells us that God took of Moses'
prophetic spirit and placed it upon seventy elders. The
result gives us insight into Paul's statement, "but
rather that ye may prophesy." These elders knew they
had Moses' spirit because they prophesied.

A prophetic leader usually has a prophetic house with
prophetic people; if they aren't trying to be a one man
show. Because Moses' spirit was on the seventy

elders, they were able to bear the burden with him and more could be accomplished. So, when Paul says, "but rather that ye may prophesy," he understands that the gift of prophecy has the ability to reach and edify more people at the same time. "For ye may all prophesy one by one that all may learn and all may be comforted" (1 Corinthians 14:31).

There were two men (Eldad and Medad), who were summoned to the tabernacle, "they were of them that were written, but they went not out unto the tabernacle: and prophesied in the camp" (Numbers 11:26). Jewish tradition suggests they didn't think themselves worthy of this blessing so they chose not to go to the tabernacle with the rest. Yet, we see that the Spirit fell on them and they prophesied in the camp. So, while there was a prophetic release taking place at the church, there was also one taking place in the camp.

Joshua went and told Moses that Eldad and Medad were prophesying in the camp; hoping he would stop them but Moses discerned his envy and stated, "Would God that ALL THE LORD'S PEOPLE were prophets, and that the Lord would put His spirit upon them" (Numbers 11:27-29).

Some, like Joshua, have tried to hinder the prophetic movement because of a zeal but not according to knowledge. Despite all the criticism and backlash the prophetic ministry receives, it is still God's heart. The last day move is a prophetic movement (Joel 2:28). Are we all prophets? No, but as Moses gives us a sneak preview of 1 Corinthians 14:1, we find that prophetic ministry was always the heart of God.

The Prophetic Movement Is A Sign That We're In the Last Days

"**28 And it shall come to pass afterward, that I will pour out my spirit upon all flesh; and your sons and your daughters shall prophesy, your old men shall dream dreams, your young men shall see visions: 29 And also upon the servants and upon the handmaids in those days will I pour out my spirit.**"

Joel 2:28-29 (KJV)

"**16 But this is that which was spoken by the prophet Joel; 17 And it shall come to pass in the last**

days, saith God, I will pour out of my Spirit upon all flesh: and your sons and your daughters shall prophesy, and your young men shall see visions, and your old men shall dream dreams: [18] **And on my servants and on my handmaidens I will pour out in those days of my Spirit; and they shall prophesy:"**

Acts 2:16-18 (KJV)

In the book of Joel, we find God contending with His people because of their sin. He commands the priests to, "blow the trumpet in Zion and to sound the alarm that the day of the Lord cometh, for it is nigh at hand" (Joel 2:1). God said He was sending a great army against His people. Then He called for Judah and Jerusalem to repent and rend their hearts, not their garments.

God said He would be jealous for His land, and pity His people (Joel 2:18). He said He would send corn, and wine, and oil as a result of their repentance. Joel 2:18-27 speaks of a revival and restoration of land that was eaten up by locusts, canker worms, and caterpillars. Then in verses 28-29 the prophet Joel shifts and begins to prophesy about a future outpour of the

Spirit which included everyone; not just prophets, kings, priests, and judges. These were those on whom the Spirit of God came and primarily used in the Old Testament.

Peter grasped this on the day of Pentecost in Acts Chapter 2. He addressed the crowd after some thought they were drunk with new wine, saying, "for these are not drunk as you suppose, seeing it is but the third hour of the day, but this is that which the prophet Joel spoke" (Acts 2:15-16).

Peter understood, by the Spirit, that prophecy was being fulfilled at that moment. At the time, Peter assumed the outpour was about and for the Jews only; that is, until he got to Cornelius' house. It was then that it became evident that it was a continuation of what happened on the day of Pentecost (Acts 10:44-45).

The main point I want to make is that the outpour represented a prophetic spirit that would be released upon everyone in the last days. The Holy Spirit is a prophetic spirit.

"¹⁷ And it shall come to pass in the last days, saith God, I will pour out of my Spirit upon all flesh: and your sons and your daughters shall prophesy, and your young men shall see visions, and your old men shall dream dreams: ¹⁸ And on my servants and on my handmaidens, I will pour out in those days of my Spirit; AND THEY SHALL PROPHESY."

Acts 2:17-18 (KJV)

Although we are not all prophets, we all have the ability to prophesy one by one. It is also important to note that, although everyone can prophesy, not everyone has the gift of prophecy as mentioned in 1 Corinthians 12:9. Some people have this gift as a manifestation of the Spirit, as He wills at a particular time and for a specific purpose.

The Bible says, Philip had four daughters who prophesied (Acts 21:9). I believe his daughters had the gift of prophecy, but some believe they were prophetesses.

The word prophesy as mentioned in Acts 21:9 means to, "foretell events, divine, speak under inspiration, exercise the prophetic office." The reason I believe they had the gift of prophecy is because a certain prophet, named Agabus, went to Philip's house, took Paul's girdle, bound his hands and feet, and said, "thus saith the Holy Ghost, so shall the Jews at Jerusalem bind the man that owneth this girdle, and shall deliver him into the hands of the Gentiles" (Acts 21:11). Paul was already in the midst of four young ladies with prophetic gifts, yet a prophet speaking with more authority, out of his office, had to go to Judea and deliver the Word of the Lord to Paul. I'm not saying this is the case, but it appears that God wanted to use the office of a prophet to deliver the message. I could be wrong, but it's something to think about.

My First Real Personal Experience with the Gift of Prophecy.

Over twenty years ago, when I was a young minister of the Gospel, I recall ministering to a congregation about Daniel in the lions' den. There was a young lady there upon whom the Lord fastened my eyes. Before I knew it, I began prophesying to her. I had previously prophesied in worship services, both corporately and personally, but this was different. I immediately knew that the gift of prophecy as mentioned in 1 Corinthians 12:9 was at work.

"7 But the manifestation of the Spirit is given to every man to profit withal. 8 For to one is given by the Spirit the word of wisdom; to another the word of knowledge by the same Spirit;"

1 Corinthians 12:7-8 (KJV)

At that moment, the gift of prophecy was given by the Spirit as a manifestation to profit withal. On that night the gift of prophecy was given to profit that young lady. It was as if the Lord burst out of me. She wept and cried under the power of God and after the service, she confirmed every word.

There were other times when I flowed out of my office and accurately prophesied, but it wasn't the same operation of the Spirit.

"And there are diversities of operation (an effect working), but it is the same God which worketh all in all."

1 Corinthians 12:6 (KJV)

"But he that prophesieth speaketh unto men to edification, and exhortation, and comfort."

1 Corinthians 14:3 (KJV)

The previous scripture shows us that the second realm of the prophetic speaks to men for three specific purposes: **edification**, **exhortation**, and **comfort**. Keeping this in mind, I believe it is safe to say that this realm of the prophetic has parameters to it. However, we must remember that God is God and can do whatever He desires. With that being said, the gift of prophecy's scope is to edify, exhort, and comfort. In other words, when receiving prophetic ministry in this realm, the aforementioned shall be its effect on a person's life.

People with the gift of prophecy are not necessarily prophets operating out of an office. The prophetic office is broader in its function. Prophets have the ability to steer the church in a particular direction. They rebuke, correct, and prophesy for edification, exhortation, and comfort. Prophecy is a powerful gift to the Body of Christ because it builds people up.

In Strong's Concordance # G3619, the word "edification" means: architecture, concretely, a structure; figuratively, confirmation, building. When the gift of prophecy goes forth, it is like an architect designing and constructing buildings. Prophecy builds our faith and gives a structure where hope can live. Edification given through prophecy causes believers to hope against hope. That is, to cling to a possibility.

God made a promise (gave a prophecy) to Abraham that he would be the father of many nations.

"(As it is written, I have made thee a father of many nations), before him whom he believed, even God, who quickeneth the dead and calleth those things which be not as though they were. Who against hope he believed in hope."

Romans 4:17-18 (KJV)

Abraham was an old man when God promised he would have an heir from his own loins (Genesis 15:4). Romans 4:17-20 says:

"[17](As it is written, I have made thee a father of many nations,) before him whom he believed,

even God, who quickeneth the dead, and calleth those things which be not as though they were. [18] Who against hope believed in hope, that he might become the father of many nations, according to that which was spoken, So shall thy seed be. [19] And being not weak in faith, he considered not his own body now dead, when he was about an hundred years old, neither yet the deadness of Sarah's womb: [20] He staggered not at the promise of God through unbelief; but was strong in faith, giving glory to God;"

Through prophecy, Abraham's faith was edified. Prophecy made him hope against the obvious and natural order of things. Prophecy was an architect, designing and constructing Abraham's vision beyond what he saw. The promise (prophecy) gave him hope against his reality. As a result, his faith was strengthened and he was able to stay built up beyond his own body; which was dead. This also applied to the deadness of Sarah's womb. Because his spirit was built up, he didn't consider his reality at that time.

When men have not been edified, all they consider is their present problems. However, when the gift of prophecy goes forth, men are lifted up from despair, unbelief, and doubt. Prophecy confirms men and women in their resolve. Can you imagine an army of built up saints who are edified in their faith? That's why the devil hates prophecy, and that's why we all need to be trained and activated in this gift to some degree.

It is hard to remain discouraged while in a prophetic house (environment), surrounded by prophetic people. There were many times when God used people with this gift to build me up. I recall times when, as a young believer, I wanted to quit and throw in the towel, but God would use someone operating in the gift of prophecy to give me hope. It was a word fitly spoken that broke despair off my life.

Jonathan's Edification to David in the Woods

"16 And Jonathan Saul's son arose, and went to David into the wood, and strengthened his hand in God. 17 And he said unto him, Fear not: for the hand of Saul my father shall not find thee; and thou shalt be king over Israel, and I shall be next unto thee; and that also Saul my father knoweth.

¹⁸ And they two made a covenant before the L<small>ORD</small>: and David abode in the wood, and Jonathan went to his house."

1 Samuel 23:16:18 (KJV)

To give you a little background, David was on the run from Saul, the first king over Israel. God rejected Saul as king in 1 Samuel 15 and in chapter 16, Samuel was instructed to go down to Jesse's house and anoint one of his sons to be the next king over Israel; that turned out to be David. King Saul became jealous of David and tried to kill him, but David escaped and ran for his life. He became a fugitive.

King Saul had a son, named Jonathan, who over the course of time, became David's greatest friend. According to the Bible, at Jonathan's funeral, David said that Jonathan's love for him "passed that of a woman" (2 Samuel 1:26). Now that I have given you a little history let's get to the crux of what I want to share.

David was running from King Saul and hiding out in caves, but remember, he was anointed to be the next king over Israel. He had prophecy over his life, but he was running for his life. He had been anointed king, but he was being hunted like a dog.

When you have a promise over your life, oftentimes you will have to live in two realities. One is the promise you carry in your heart. The other is the reality that Saul is pursuing you every day. Saul will eventually fade away as your prophecy and your promise take precedence.

After time and process had run its course, the Bible says, "Jonathan went to David into the wood and strengthened his hand in God" (1 Samuel 23:16). Jonathan's name means: Jehovah gives, bestows, adds, distributes. Prophecy is one of those gifts that meets you in the woods of despair, depression, and doubt. It gives, bestows, and adds to your faith.

Jonathan was the king's son, living in a palace, yet he left his comfortability and went into the woods to edify and comfort David. The scripture says, "Jonathan strengthened his hand in God" (1 Samuel 23:16)."

Strengthened is the Hebrew word **"chazaq"** (Strong's Concordance #H2388). It means to be strong, cure, repair, fortify, and confirm, just to name a few.

Jonathan went to the woods to prophesy to David that he might be cured, repaired, and confirmed. Jonathan wasn't a prophet but we cannot deny that this is definitely the gift of prophecy in operation, for the purpose of building David's faith, while he was in the woods waiting on prophecy to be fulfilled. I believe Jonathan was repairing and confirming David's spirit and faith in God. No doubt he was tired, frustrated, and perplexed about his life and about his prophetic destiny. Now let's look at what Jonathan said to strengthen his hand in God.

"And he said unto him, Fear not: for the hand of Saul my father shall not find thee; and thou shalt be king over Israel, and I shall be next unto thee; and that also Saul my father knoweth."

1 Samuel 23:17 (KJV)

There are 3 things I want you to grab hold of from this scripture:

1. **Fear not:** The gift of prophecy eradicates fear when it is administered.

2. **My father shall not find thee:** Prophecy confirmed his protection.

3. **And thou shalt be king over Israel:** This
    prophecy confirmed the previous prophecy.

As a result of the gift of prophecy being in operation
David's faith was repaired, strengthened, and
confirmed by his friend, Jonathan.

Oftentimes, when we're in the woods of life, the gift of
prophecy serves as a light that strengthens our hand
in God. It repairs and builds us back up in our faith.

Prophecy exhorts us as well. The word exhort means,
"solace, entreaty, and comfort. It also means, "to call
near."

The Gift of Prophecy Warns Us and Calls Us Near to the Will of God to Obey Him

"9 Now when much time was spent, and when
sailing was now dangerous, because the fast was
now already past, Paul admonished them, 10 And
said unto them, Sirs, I perceive that this voyage
will be with hurt and much damage, not only of the
lading and ship, but also of our lives."

Acts 27:9-10 (KJV)

In this passage of scripture, the Apostle Paul was a prisoner on a ship headed to Italy. Sailing had become dangerous and Paul perceived (by the Spirit) that the voyage would result in hurt and much damage of the lading and the ship, and more importantly, of their lives.

Prophecy also serves as an exhortation to warn and propel us to obey God. It calls us nearer to the will of God for our lives. When we obey God's exhortations, we preserve ourselves and those who are connected to us. Sometimes the gift of prophecy serves to protect us from hurt and damage.

Prophecy Comforts Us

"**20 And when neither sun nor stars in many days appeared, and no small tempest lay on us, all hope that we should be saved was then taken away. 21 But after long abstinence Paul stood forth in the midst of them, and said, Sirs, ye should have hearkened unto me, and not have loosed from Crete, and to have gained this harm and loss. 22 And now I exhort you to be of good cheer: for there shall be no loss of any man's life among you,** but of the ship. [23] For there stood by me this night the angel of God, whose I am, and whom I serve, [24] Saying, Fear not, Paul; thou must be brought before Caesar: and, lo, God hath given thee all them that sail with thee."

Acts 27:20-24 (KJV)

"Comfort ye, comfort ye my people saith your God."

Isaiah40:1 (KJV)

Once again, as a prisoner, Paul was headed to Italy, and after having warned the centurion about the danger that laid ahead, they disregarded him and decided to continue on their journey. As a result, they found themselves in a hopeless situation; with neither sun nor stars appearing after many days (Acts 27:20). After this long abstinence, the Bible says, Paul stood forth in the midst of them and began to give the Word of the Lord (Acts 27:21). He began to comfort them with the comfort wherewith he was comforted by God (2 Corinthians 1:4).

"[23] For there stood by me this night the angel of God, whose I am, and whom I serve, [24] Saying, Fear

**not, Paul; thou must be brought before Caesar:
and, lo, God hath given thee all them that sail with
thee. ²⁵ Wherefore, sirs, be of GOOD CHEER: for I
believe God, that it shall be even as it was told me."**

Acts 27:23-25 (KJV)

Paul received a Word from an angel that everyone
would be saved. He was reassured that there would be
no loss except the ship. Great comfort is given to those
who are visited with prophecy, whether it comes
through a handmaiden, a servant, an angel, or a
prophet. God's comfort is the same, regardless of the
new covenant administration or operation. Through
prophecy we are graced to, "comfort ye, comfort ye
God's people." This includes those who live outside of
the new covenant of Jesus Christ.

❧ CHAPTER THREE ❧

"The Office of the Prophet/Prophetess"

A prophet is simply, a divinely inspired spokesperson for God. They reveal God's mind and purposes for individuals, churches, governments, etc... It is only by God's sovereign call and election that one is brought into this office.

"Before I formed thee in the belly, I knew thee; and before thou camest forth out of the womb I sanctified thee, and I ordained thee a prophet unto the nations."

Jeremiah 1:5 (KJV)

No man can make you a prophet. God ordained Jeremiah a prophet unto the nations before he was formed in his mother's womb. In the New Testament, a prophet is an ascension gift to the Body of Christ (Ephesians 1:8-13). The gift of the prophet is not a gift of the Holy Spirit (1 Corinthians 12:7), but rather an extension of Jesus Christ; as a prophet Himself. Through the five-fold ministry gifts of the church, the

Apostle, the Prophet, the Evangelist, the Pastor, and the Teacher, Christ has broken Himself into five-parts to express His headship to the church (Ephesians 4:11).

When these ministry gifts operate in full maturity, they express the revealing of Christ in perfecting the saints for the work of the ministry, and for edifying the Body of Christ. Although prophets have many functions in ministry, the primary role of the prophet in the New Testament church is to equip the church. We've already discussed the gift of prophecy and its purpose; however, the ministry of the prophet covers more ground and has a greater responsibility than those who just prophesy. Let's examine this in greater detail.

Prophets don't just prophesy; they correct, rebuke and give direction to the church. When Israel got off course, God would send a prophet to realign them and move them back into His purpose. When Israel wouldn't listen to those prophets, they would always end up shipwrecked.

As we receive prophets in the name of prophets, we receive a prophet's reward (Matthew 10:41). Prophets are strong in giving direction to assist people on what to do and what not to do for their success. They operate strongly in the "word of wisdom." The gift of wisdom is not prophecy as most think; they are not the same. The word of wisdom shows you how to fulfill prophecy and can be given in the form of instruction. Once obeyed, it can lead to great success or accomplishment. At your leisure read 2 Kings 5:10-14 and 2 Kings 4:1-7.

"And the elders of the Jews builded, and they _prospered_ through the prophesying of Haggai the prophet and Zechariah, the son of Iddo. And they builded, and finished it, according to the commandment of the God of Israel, and according to the commandment of Cyrus, and Darius, and Artaxerxes king of Persia"

Ezra 6:14 (KJV)

In the days of Ezra, the people prospered and were able to finish the temple through the direction of the prophets who were prophesying. The word prosper means to: "advance, to breakout, or to push forward."

When pastors won't release their prophets to prophesy and saints don't receive prophetic ministry, the completion of assignments is prolonged and many forfeit the prophet's reward. I have visited churches and have given Holy Spirit directives to pastors, and as they received it, they received a prophet's reward.

Prophets also flow strongly in revelation knowledge. They are graced to reveal God's heart and plans to the Body of Christ (Ephesians 3:3-5). Prophets flow strongly in revealing the mystery of Christ or the Word of God to the church.

There are two New Testament Greek words translated from the English language "Word." They are **Logos** and **Rhema**. Logos is referenced in 2 Timothy 2:15 and John 1:1. It refers to something said, or thought, a divine expression, or account. Logos is the infallible, complete, and life-giving Word of God. Every other expression of God or revelation must be judged by it.

In contrast, Rhema, is that word in the middle of a Word. At least, that's what I call it. Ezekiel saw a vision of a wheel in the middle of a wheel (Ezekiel 1:16). I believe Rhema is that wheel in the middle of Logos; the written Word that we get a word from. All believers have access to this, but prophets who are mature have the eyes of their understanding enlightened on another level, for the purpose of bringing present day truth to the church (2 Peter 1:12).

Jesus was and is the Word (logos), made flesh, (rhema) who dwelt among us (John 1:14). Remember, Jesus said, "Man shall not live by bread alone, but by every word:" utterance, matter or topic, a pouring forth" (Strong's # G4487 from 4483), "that proceedeth (comes forth) out of the mouth of God."

When Abraham was instructed to sacrifice his son, the first word he received was, "sacrifice your son," but then he received a second word from the angel of the Lord who, "called unto him out of heaven," and told him to, "stay his hand" (Genesis 22:1-12). If Abraham had not been living from every word that **proceedeth** out of the mouth of God, he would have killed his promise.

Logos is the written Word, but Rhema is what is being revealed from the scriptures by revelation or illumination. I believe we must have God's mind operating in our lives to be seasoned and strong prophets.

1 Corinthians 12 lists various gifts of the Spirit. There are three I want to specifically mention. The word of wisdom, the word of knowledge, and the discerning of spirits. These are revelatory gifts in that they are gifts that reveal.

Most seasoned prophets I know operate very strongly in at least two of these three gifts. These are some of the ways in which prophets are able to reveal; through preaching, teaching, and prophesying. Prophets have visited my church and revealed the devil's devices, expressed God's desire for us as a ministry, and exposed hinderances that were in our way. I have visited other churches and done the same.

The prophet Elisha told the King of Israel not to pass by a certain place, and as he obeyed, his life was saved. The King of Syria's heart was troubled by this, so he called his servants and asked, "who is on the king of Israel's side?" One of his servants responded, "none my lord oh king, but Elisha the prophet, that is in Israel telleth the king of Israel the words that thou speaketh in thy bedchamber" (2 Kings 6:1-12).

You see, prophets are hated because we don't just reveal God's plans, we also expose the works of Satan, bringing him to an open shame. Prophets are hated by the kingdom of darkness.

God sets prophets over nations and regions to root out, to pull down, to destroy, to throw down, to build, and to plant (Jeremiah 1:10).

The prophetic anointing roots out:
A prophet's anointing deals with the root of things; they are strong in rooting out the works of the enemy. John the Baptist, who was a prophet, bore witness to this function in the New Testament when he said, "And now also the axe is laid to the root of the trees: therefore, every tree which bringeth not forth good fruit is hewn down, and cast into the fire" (Matthew 3:10).

Jeremiah was anointed to root out; tear away, forsake, pluck out, up by the roots, and pull up. I've prophesied to people across the country, and seen God root out spirits and lay the axe to the root of things that wouldn't allow them to bear fruit. The prophetic anointing often does its work in the secret parts of an individual's life where bitterness and unforgiveness lies undetected. This type of anointing goes after demons lying in secret places.

The prophetic anointing pulls down:
Beats down, breaks down, destroys, and overthrows. Prophets beat and break down demonic strongholds over time. Prophets pull down strongholds over nations, regions, cities, churches, and families. We are anointed to destroy and overthrow the works of the devil through prophesying, teaching, and preaching.

The prophetic anointing destroys:
Prophets also destroy: to wander away, lose oneself, to perish, to be void. Prophets teach and preach in a way that makes you lose your life to follow Christ. Jesus said, "if you lose your life, you will find it" (Matthew 10:39). Again, prophets destroy that which is not of God.

The prophetic anointing throws down:
Prophets are also anointed to throw down: to pull down or in pieces, to beat down or through. Prophets are anointed to violently throw down systems and kingdoms that have been established in our lives.

The prophetic anointing builds and plants:

Prophets also build and plant. The word build here means: "to begin to build, builder, to obtain children, make, repair, and set up." Prophets are anointed to activate believers in their callings and giftings. We open spiritual wombs for others to give birth on so many levels. We establish people in the faith; then we plant (to strike in or fasten).

❧ CHAPTER FOUR ❧

"Growing Prophets"

Prophets are born then made through growth and the process of time. We know through scripture that God said Jeremiah was a prophet before he was formed in his mother's womb, yet he received the call as a young man. Some believe it was at the age of seventeen. Scripture does not give us details into his process or maturation as a prophet, but we know he was a child when he responded to the call (Jeremiah 1:4-7). We should also note that he came from a family of priests.

Jesus' whole mission, from eternity past, was to do the Father's will. The Bible says He was the, "lamb of God, slain **before** the foundation of the world" (Revelation 13:8). The Bible also says, "when the fullness of time was come, God sent forth His Son, made of a woman, born under the law" (Galatians 4:4). Philippians 2:5-8 explains how Jesus laid aside His heavenly glory and took upon Him the form of a servant and was made in the likeness of men.

It was prophesied in Isaiah 7:14 that Jesus would be born of a virgin and that she would name the child Immanuel (God is with us). Matthew 1:18-25 tells us, He would be called the son of Joseph but He would be conceived of the Holy Ghost.

"And the child grew and waxed strong in the spirit, filled with wisdom: and the grace of God was upon him."

Luke 2:40 (KJV)

"And Jesus increased in wisdom and stature, and in favour with God and with man."

Luke 2:52 (KJV)

"And Jesus matured, growing up in body and in spirit, blessed by both God and people."

Luke 2:52 (MSG)

"And the child grew, and waxed strong in spirit, and was in the deserts till the day of his showing unto Israel."

Luke 1:80 (KJV)

There are stages and certain processes every prophet has to go through. Prophets are ordained of God, but made through sonship and training.

Before Jesus' disciples were called apostles, they were disciples (Matthew 10:1-2). They had to follow Jesus for three and a half years, learning and observing their teacher. "And he said to them, Follow me, and I will **make** you fishers of men" (Matthew 4:19). Following makes you become a thing; if you follow the right way. Prophets beget prophets.

There are three realms to a prophet's growth. The child prophet, the adolescent prophet, and the adult prophet. It is important that I point out that the anointing and gifts are given by the Holy Spirit and not necessarily because of growth. Gifts come with the Holy Spirit, but maturity and character are the result of time and experience. To put it another way, we could say 30, 60, and 100-fold prophets.

Speaking of Jesus, the Bible says, "the **child** grew, and waxed strong in spirit, filled with wisdom: and the grace of God was upon him" (Luke 2:40). Because Jesus is the son of man too, He had to take on the nature and humanity of man as well.

"He took upon Him the form of a servant and was made in the likeness of men."

Philippians 2:7 (KJV)

Even Jesus had to grow up naturally and spiritually. You see, a **child** was born in Bethlehem, but a **son** was given at the Jordan river when He submitted to John's Baptism to fulfill all righteousness (Isaiah 7:14; Matthew 3:13-17).

When it comes to growth, healthy children should be growing mentally, emotionally, and physically. Spiritual people, specifically prophets (for the sake of this book), should be growing in like manner, with increase or growth to their spirit, their level of wisdom, their stature (maturity), and in grace (Luke 2:52). There are several specific areas I want us to examine from the life of Jesus, that will help us better understand how prophets grow and identify the areas in which they grow. The first area we will examine is:

Jesus waxed strong in the spirit (Luke 2:40).
Growing prophets should be waxing strong in the Spirit. To wax strong in the spirit is to increase in vigor (be strengthened, strong); to be powerful in

Christ's Spirit, vital principal, mental disposition (superhuman), and spiritually minded.

Remember, Paul tells us to, "be strong in the Lord and in the power of his might" (Ephesians 6:10). Prophets are to be strengthened with might by the Spirit in the inner man (Ephesians 3:16). The inner man of a prophet has to be developed through intimacy with the Holy Spirit, prayer, fasting, much Word intake, and the trials of life.

Prophets wax strong in the Spirit when they "walk worthy of the Lord unto all pleasing, being fruitful in every good work and increasing in the knowledge of God: strengthened with all might, according to His glorious power, unto all patience and longsuffering with joyfulness" (Colossians 1:10-11).

The more a young prophet walks worthy of the Lord unto all pleasing, being fruitful in every good work, they become strengthened with all might, ever coming to know God more and more. Their inner man becomes stronger and stronger.

Prophets also grow in the Spirit when they exercise their spiritual senses by reason of use (Hebrews 5:14). Faith is like a muscle that needs to be exercised to get bigger and stronger. Through the use of our gifts, faith, and our obedient responses to God, we are empowered by the Spirit and able to discern spiritual things more accurately.

The second area we will examine is:

Jesus was filled with wisdom (Luke 2:40; 2:52).

Prophets must grow in wisdom. The Bible says, "wisdom is justified of her children" (Luke 7:35). In this text, the definition of wisdom means: "thoughtful, sagacious, or discreet, acumen." James 3:17 talks about the wisdom that is from above. Most young prophets who don't have this wisdom wonder why pastors won't invite them to speak at their churches. They fail to realize that, although they may hear from God, they don't possess the wisdom of God to accommodate or articulate His message. In some settings, knowing how to say something is more important than saying or releasing it.

We see the wisdom of a prophet in operation when Nathan confronted and prophesied to David concerning his affair with Bathsheba and the death of Uriah (2 Samuel 11; 12:1-4). The prophet Nathan gave the word, but he did so in wisdom. He respected the king by using a parable, so as not to provoke the king's wrath or pride.

Wisdom, or a lack thereof is revealed by what comes out of your mouth, and more importantly, how it comes out. Prophets must learn to exalt wisdom and it will bring them to honor (Proverbs 4:8). How you understand things reveals your level of wisdom. Paul taught that immaturity is revealed by how we understand. "When I was a child, I spake as a child, I understood as a child, I thought as a child: but when I became a man, I put away childish things" (1 Corinthians 13:11). Wisdom is also revealed in how we conduct ourselves.

I've seen prophets, both young and old, with no personal or relational skills. I have a friend who is mighty in the scriptures and is a very strong prophet, but he lacks the wisdom to be relational. He has no personality. Body language and mannerisms have a lot to do with wisdom. Your countenance and body language speaks louder than you think.

The wisdom of God is easily intreated (James 3:17). Prophets must know how to wisely go in and out amongst diversities of people (1 Samuel 18:5).

The third area we will examine is:

Prophets grow in grace (Luke 2:40).

In this passage of scripture, grace is translated in the Greek as, "**charis:** khar'ece (Strong's Concordance #G5485). It means graciousness, of manner or act, the divine influence upon the heart, favour, grace, and liberality. The Bible says we are to "grow in grace and in the knowledge of our Lord and savior Jesus Christ (2 Peter 3:18). We are told that Jesus grew in the grace of God. Likewise, prophets must grow in grace, or in God's divine influence upon their lives. This grace is seen as the presence of God increasing on them. It grows more and more, causing prophets to be more spiritually and divinely influenced by God.

As a young prophet, God's grace grew on me to the point that people could recognize it. Grace can be seen and heard (Galatians 2:9). "And Samuel **grew**, and the

Lord was with him, and did let none of his words fall to the ground. And ALL Israel from Dan even to Beersheba knew that Samuel was **established** to be a prophet of the Lord" (1 Samuel 3:19-20).

Samuel grew in the grace and knowledge of the Lord and people saw that growth. Paul told Timothy not to neglect the gift he had and that he was to meditate (take care of, revolve in the mind, premeditate) upon it, giving himself wholly (entirely) to it that his profiting (progress) may appear to all men (1 Timothy 4:15).

Prophets who don't grow in the grace and knowledge of Jesus Christ become weak and title prophets by name rather than by the grace and knowledge of Jesus Christ. To be strong prophets we have to **know** Jesus by His Word and His Spirit.

After 60 years of ministry, Paul was still crying out, "Oh! That I may know Him…" (Philippians 3:8-10). We must follow on to **know** the Lord each and every single day (Hosea 6:3).

From time to time, grace (divine influence) was seen moving upon Sampson in the camp of Dan between

Zorah and Eshtaol (Judges 13:25). Grace was seen growing on the young Sampson.

The fourth area we will examine is:

Prophets Must Grow In Stature (Maturity).

The Bible says, "Jesus grew in stature" (Luke 2:52). Stature is maturity or maturation. God takes His time growing His prophets into mature prophets. It takes years to mature as a full-grown prophet. Many prophets have broken rank and process because they had a gift. They broke rank only to realize that they failed to stay in their father or mothers' house long enough to be cooked on the inside. Hosea said, "Israel is a half-baked cake" (Hosea 7:8). Many prophets' gifts got done, but their character remained undone. The result is always the same; a gift with no substance and a messenger without the Lord's message (Haggai 1:13).

Maturity comes from humility, obedience, service, trials, and most importantly, waiting on your ministry. I will deal with this in a later chapter.

❧ CHAPTER FIVE ❧

"Prophetic Fathering/Mentorship"

"And the child Samuel ministered unto the LORD before Eli. And the word of the LORD was precious in those days; there was no open vision."

1 Samuel 3:1 (KJV)

Before I begin expounding on this chapter, let me bring a little clarity to the term prophetic fathering and mentorship. In a natural relationship between a father and a son, the father has a responsibility to develop that son through love, chastisement, correction, guidance, and wisdom. A father should create a safe environment for a child to grow and express themselves so that talents, gifts, and skill sets can be honed over a period of time.

Samuel represents a type of prophetic fathering.

"And Saul sent messengers to take David: and when they saw the company of the prophets prophesying, and Samuel <u>standing as appointed</u>

over them, the Spirit of God was upon the messengers of Saul, and they also prophesied"

1 Samuel 19:20 (KJV)

Paul said, "If you have ten thousand guardians in Christ, you do not have many fathers; for in Christ Jesus I became your father through the gospel" (1 Corinthians 4:15 NIV). Timothy was a son to Paul because Paul watched over his spiritual life and helped develop his character and gifts over time. (1 Timothy 1:2). Elijah fathered and mentored prophets; notably Elisha (2 Kings 1-2; 4:38-44).

Prophetic fathering is creating a relational atmosphere where sons and daughters can grow in their gifts and callings. It is taking the time to nurture them and providing hands on training, while standing over them; as Samuel did. Mentorship is defined as the guidance provided by a mentor, especially an experienced person in a company or educational institution.

With the rise and popularity of prophetic ministry, if we ever needed prophetic fathering and mentorship, we need it now! You see, if an individuals' relationship with Christ is unscriptural or off, their relationship as a prophet or prophetic person will be off as well. Prophetic fathering/mentorship gives us a real-life pattern to look at and follow; other than those we read about in the Bible. Jesus is our pattern as a son, Apostle, Prophet, Pastor, Evangelist, and Teacher. The Apostle Paul is the template that shows us what it means to father sons and daughters. Let's get to the crux of this chapter.

"And the child Samuel ministered unto the Lord before Eli. And the word of the Lord was precious in those days; there was no open vision."

1 Samuel 3:1 (KJV)

For the backdrop of this text, it would serve you well to read 1 Samuel 1-2. Eli was the judge and priest over Israel during this time; his sons were priests as well. They made God's people abhor the offerings of the Lord (1 Samuel 2:22-34). God rebuked Eli for not rebuking and restraining his sons. God rebuked him yet he was still needed and necessary for the development of the young Samuel, who was on the rise.

Just because a man or woman of God has a blemish, spot, a rent garment, or a dead fly in their anointing in one season, that doesn't disqualify them from training or equipping the next generation of Samuels. Their experience is beneficial for growing Samuels. Even Eli's can recover their first love again.

The Bible says Samuel, "ministered unto the Lord **before** Eli." Young prophets and prophetic people need to serve God in the presence of senior leaders. Samuel was in the temple serving God through menial tasks so as to worship; he was learning his priestly duties. Young prophets should make themselves available to prophetic gatherings and times of corporate prayer, ministering before their prophetic father. It gives a prophetic father the chance to hear if you're growing in grace in your prayer life. It also shows accountability and humility on the part of the son or daughter.

These types of settings build prophetic confidence and spiritual discipline in a young prophet or prophetic person. Samuel ministered unto the Lord, but it was before Eli. If young prophets would live by this principle, I believe it would act as a safe guard in their spiritual lives. I've literally seen people lose their minds and become prophetic spooks because they thought God would teach them everything. In their eyes, there was no need to minister unto the Lord, **before** their prophetic father or mentor.

Sometimes a prophetic father is good for checks and balances; we can all miss it and get off at times. I am grateful for the people God placed in my life while I was growing as a prophet and ministering **before** the Lord. It has protected me from being bitten by serpents (Ecclesiastes 10:8).

Prophetic Fathering/Mentorship Helps You Identify the Dealings of God in Your Life

"³ And ere the lamp of God went out in the temple of the LORD, where the ark of God was, and Samuel was laid down to sleep; ⁴ That the LORD called Samuel: and he answered, Here am I. ⁵ And he ran unto Eli, and said, Here am I; for thou calledst me. And he said, I called not; lie down again. And he went and lay down. ⁶ And the LORD called yet again, Samuel. And Samuel arose and went to Eli, and said, Here am I; for thou didst call me. And he answered, I called not, my son; lie down again. ⁷ Now Samuel did not yet know the LORD, neither was the word of the LORD yet revealed unto him. ⁸ And the LORD called Samuel again the third time. And he arose and went to Eli, and said, Here am I; for thou didst call me. And Eli perceived that the LORD had called the child. ⁹ Therefore Eli said unto Samuel, Go, lie down: and it shall be, if he call thee, that thou shalt say, Speak, LORD; for thy servant heareth. So, Samuel went and lay down in his place. ¹⁰ And the LORD came, and stood, and called as at other times, Samuel, Samuel. Then Samuel answered, Speak; for thy servant heareth."

1 Samuel 3:3-10 (KJV)

God spoke to Samuel three times, as mentioned in the previous scriptures. Samuel kept hearing something but it sounded like Eli to him. I recall as a young prophet, hearing my Apostle's voice in a dream or in my spirit. It was what I could relate to in my formative years while learning the voice of God. I was dull of hearing and my spiritual senses weren't exercised enough yet.

Like Samuel, I didn't know the Lord, neither was the Word of the Lord yet revealed unto me (Verse 7). Sons and daughters should always run to their prophetic father/mentors when they believe they've heard God speak, by way of a vision, dream, a still small voice, through the written Word, or an audible voice. There should always be seasoned five-fold ministry gifts standing over you who can accurately judge what you say you saw or heard.

Prophetic fathers are able to perceive when God is dealing with an individual or if they just have a desire operating in them that they want to be God. It is important to note, running to everybody for guidance can confuse you and circumvent your growth. Samuel ran to Eli, not Jim, Bob, Sue Bell, and Mary. Senior prophets will help you identify your gifts, activate you in those gifts, and discern your time to be released in those gifts.

Prophetic Fathering Judges What You Think You Heard or Saw

"Therefore, Eli said unto Samuel, <u>Go, lie down</u>: and it shall be, if he call thee, that thou shalt say,

Speak, Lord; for thy servant heareth. So, <u>Samuel
went and lay down in his place.</u>"

1 Samuel 3:9 (KJV)

"[20] **Despise not prophesyings.** [21] **Prove all things;
hold fast that which is good.**"

1 Thessalonians 5:20-21 (KJV)

Samuel thought Eli was calling him, but it was God.
Samuel didn't know the Lord at that time, neither had
the Word of the Lord been revealed to him. When Eli
perceived it could be God, he told Samuel, "<u>Go, lie
down</u>." Prophetic fathering and mentorship will
remove a hasty spirit from you. I remember a young
minister in my church who wanted to leave nursing
school and go do ministry. She felt it was God, but my
experience in life and knowing her as a spiritual
daughter, I knew it wasn't the will of God.

I politely said, "go lie down" (chuckles). I told her I
didn't think it was time. She submitted to my counsel
and finished her degree as a nurse. Mentorship is all
about giving other people your experience, whether
good or bad. This young lady has become a powerful
woman of God and a nurse.

Fathers should be able to judge what you say God spoke to you. One of the ways I know who's becoming a son or a daughter is when I can judge or correct what they think they heard from God. If they survive that "acid test," I've just gained a Timothy and Titus.

A few years ago, a woman who was a member of my church for a short period of time, enrolled in my School of the Prophets. She became disgruntled, after I put her up to minister in the class. She came to the ministry with the title "Prophetess." I try not to get into who's a prophet and who isn't, but the proof is in the pudding. I'll give you a mic in a small controlled setting and say, "go for it." Well, she flopped several times...

People have a way of disqualifying themselves without you ever saying a word. It was obvious her ministry needed a lot of training and development, but I knew it was going to be a challenge for her; seeing that she thought she was a prophetess already. To make matters worse, there were young, two-year old ministers at our church who were preaching and prophesying circles around her.

Out of embarrassment, she created a strife within herself to exit the ministry. One day she told me, "I don't feel loved like everybody else." She shared that she had attended a church and the pastor's wife prophesied to her that my wife didn't like her. So, I said to her, "let's judge and prove the word." I asked, "what is the fruit that my wife has an ought with you? She is just as kind and loving to you as she is to everyone else." We proved to her if she really did get a prophecy, as she'd stated, there was no fruit to it. We later found out she had told them she was receiving a lump sum of money, and they went to work on her, prophesying her out of the church she belonged to.

The point here is, she wouldn't **"go lie down."** The end result was that she was deceived and uprooted out of a ministry that, had she humbled herself, could have helped her grow in her ministry. Prophetic fathers don't allow you to be deceived or grow wrong in their presence. They make you prove all things and hold fast to that which is good (1 Thessalonians 5:21).

Following and Obeying Your
Prophetic Father/Mentor

"My son, give me thine heart, and let thine eyes observe my ways."

Proverbs 23:26 (KJV)

"And he saith unto them, Follow me, and I will make you fishers of men."

Matthew 4:19 (KJV)

"Be ye followers of me, even as I also am also of Christ."

1 Corinthians 11:1 (KJV)

"Be imitators of me, just as I also am of Christ."

1 Corinthians 11:1 (NASB)

Sons and daughters, those of prophetic houses in particular, must learn how to give their hearts to their prophetic father. I'm not referring to some occultic or perverted way, but in a godly way. Covenant must be cut in the heart and spirit. Every form of relationship needs a level of trust for individuals to benefit from one another the right way. I've seen fathers run their spiritual sons and daughters away because they were hurt or betrayed by another spiritual son or daughter. As a result of their hurt, some do ministry trying to avoid and prevent pain. Rather than raising up spiritual sons and daughters, they become too busy trying to snuff out Judas and Demas (2 Timothy 4:10).

In this line of work, being forsaken and betrayed is inevitable. I tell leaders all the time, our job is to raise them up and commend them to the Lord. We don't always know who is going to turn out to be a Timothy or Judas. Spiritual fathers care deeply for the sons and daughters entrusted to them. They don't just share the gospel; they share their lives (1 Thessalonians 2:8).

In contrast, there are times when sons and daughters are hurt by leaders and, let me add, prophetic leaders at that. Regardless of how we choose to look at it, we must understand that humanity is frail. We must trust God to lead us, and if we get hurt, to heal us. When purpose is fulfilled, we will say like David, "It was good that I was afflicted" (Psalm 119:71).

Trusting your prophetic father/mentor with your heart enables you to receive on a deeper level. When the heart is open and receptive it can attend to the things of God without distraction. In addition, you follow your man or woman of God better (Acts 16:14).

After his inauguration, the first King of Israel had a band of men, whose heart God had touched, follow him home (1 Samuel 10:26). There is power in following your prophetic father/mentor. Jesus called twelve disciples and then ordained them to be apostles (Matthew 10). Before their promotion to apostleship, they had to be students, pupils, or disciples (learned or trained ones). They all had to make the decision to follow Christ.

Jesus said, "If you follow me, I will make you a fisher of men" (Matthew 4:19). Peter and his fishing partner knew how to fish; they followed their fathers into the family business. Jesus was saying, in order to learn this trade, you will have to leave what you've been following.

The Bible says, God took Amos as he followed the flock (Amos 7:15). Someone reading this book can feel God taking you from some things you've been following. He's doing it so you can start walking in your destiny. I tell people all the time, "you become what you follow." Jesus said, "follow me, observe me, come see where I live" (Matthew 4:19). Following and observing the ways of a man or woman of God is priceless.

While living in Georgia, whenever I preached or held conferences, I always wanted our ministers there; especially our young ones. There is so much to learn when following and observing your spiritual leaders. Jesus said he could do nothing of Himself, but what He saw the Father do (John 5:19). Following and observing causes you to grow in leaps and bounds.

As we have taken observation and inventory over the years, those who gave their hearts and observed our ways have brought forth much fruit in their lives, gifts, and in their callings. I could have gone to any church and sat under any pastor and I still would have been an Apostle because that's who God made me, but I truly believe I would not be operating and flowing in the strength of my apostolic and prophetic call, as I am now, had I not submitted to my Apostle and the leaders God placed in my life.

I pray in the Spirit for hours because I had an Apostle who did it. I write books and have a strong media presence because I followed and observed that. I believe I preached at my Apostles' church once or twice, but I wasn't there for that. I was there to watch him and to support his vision. When I relocated to North Carolina he prophesied to me saying, "God says you've gotten all you needed from here." I imitated my leaders in my formative years. I cut my teeth in their ministries.

Imitation is a part of growth and development. Children grow and develop through imitation. Paul said, "follow me as I imitate Christ" (1 Corinthians 11:1). The word follow in this scripture means to, "mimic." Children mimic their parents to learn language and words. I learned how to pray and sing in the spirit imitating what I saw. We have Jesus to look to but God knew we needed a template or examples here on earth to help us mature and develop as His true sons. So, He gave gifts unto men (Ephesians 4:11).

❧ CHAPTER SIX ❧

"Prophetic Purity"

Unfortunately, the prophetic office and ministry has been reduced to something carnal and lucrative. The prophet's office is no longer upheld as sacred, and there have been many wolves in sheep's clothing and charlatans who have desecrated it. Many have aspired for this lofty office who were not called; and therein lies most of the problem, but I believe God is restoring purity back to the prophetic office and ministry.

"8 But, The LORD liveth, which brought up and which led the seed of the house of Israel out of the north country, and from all countries whither I had driven them; and they shall dwell in their own land. 9 Mine heart within me is broken because of the prophets; all my bones shake; I am like a drunken man, and like a man whom wine hath overcome, because of the LORD, and because of the words of his holiness. 10 For the land is full of adulterers; for because of swearing the land mourneth; the pleasant places of the wilderness are dried up, and their course is evil, and their

force is not right. ¹¹ For both prophet and priest are profane; yea, in my house have I found their wickedness, saith the LORD."

Jeremiah 23:8-11 (KJV)

Jeremiah, is called the "weeping prophet" because he lamented over the state of God's people. The difficulties he encountered as described in the book of Jeremiah and Lamentations have prompted scholars to refer to him as the weeping prophet.

In the preceding scripture, Jeremiah was weeping because of the prophets. The lack of zeal for God's house and the people was consuming him; and so were the prophets. I believe there are weeping prophets, like Jeremiah, who's hearts are broken because of the prophets of our day. Jeremiah was hurt because the holiness (a sacred place, dedicated things, consecrated), of God's Word was no longer being upheld or reverenced. Perverting God's words are the most dangerous coming from prophets. The prophets in Jeremiah's day diluted to Word of the Lord with mixture and compromise. Notice the Bible doesn't call them false prophets, but it is obvious they had lost their purity and consecration to the Lord.

When prophets and the prophetic ministry loses its purity, it always results in the spirit of adultery being released to the Body of Christ. Prophets who have been seduced through prosperity, fame, or the lust of the world are open to deception (John 2:15-16). When a man or woman's life goes wrong, their doctrine usually follows shortly thereafter.

The Bible teaches, we are not to plow with an ox, or an ass, or wear diverse garments (Deuteronomy 22:10-11). When a prophet loses a single eye and heart for God and His church, they start operating out of duality; preaching, prophesying, and doing ministry from two fountains, claiming to be messengers of the Lord but without the Lord's message (Haggai 1:13).

Prophets who lose their purity carry a spirit of adultery in their hearts. Adultery is more than someone going outside of their marriage covenant. It also means to "dilute something from its purest form." Mixing clean with unclean, holy with unholy, being hot nor cold as believers. Lukewarm Christianity has become the norm for most believers (Revelation 3:16). Many have a form of godliness but deny the power thereof (2 Timothy 3:5).

The Bible says, "For the land is full of adulterers; for because of swearing the land mourneth; the pleasant places of the wilderness are dried up, and their course is evil, and their force is not right" (Jeremiah 23:10).

In Jeremiah's day, as a result of the prophetic losing its purity, the spirit of adultery was released in the land. The prophets lost their way and the gifts that were supposed to reveal the heart of God and point the people to Him had become polluted.

Apostasy in the heart of prophets means apostasy in the heart of the people. "The prophet's prophesy falsely and the priests bear rule by their means; and my people love to have it so: and what will you do in the end thereof?" (Jeremiah 5:31). Hosea 4:9 says, "like people, like priest."

When leaders get off track and remain there without repentance it affects the Body of Christ. If the blind lead the blind, we all fall in a ditch (Matthew 15:14). Remember, prophetic ministry gives instruction, whether it be right or wrong. That's why the devil works overtime to pervert a prophet of God.

Notice verse 11 says, "the land was mourning and the pleasant places of the wilderness was dried up" (Jeremiah 23:10). Famine was in their land, the Spirit of the Lord had departed, and no one had repented with godly sorrow (2 Corinthians 7:10). Their course or race had become evil and their force (power, strength, might) was not right.

Many claimed to have power, vision, and dreams but their force was not right. That was the indictment against the prophets and priests of Jeremiah's day. They were profane (to soil; especially in a moral sense, corrupt, defiled, and polluted).

"yea, in my house have I found their wickedness, saith the LORD."

Jeremiah 23:11

The prophets of our day have lost their moral compass. They have corrupted themselves through greed, power, and by degenerating morally, all while profaning the sacred office and being God's mouth piece. Many have perverted this sacred office for filthy lucre (1 Timothy 3:8). Their god has become their belly (Philippians 3:19).

Notice, the Bible says both prophet and priest have become profane. Every prophet should have a priestly ministry; one in which they offer spiritual sacrifices unto God. It is under sacred pretention and religious pious that both are profaned right in God's house.

Their wickedness was found in God's house. The priests in the holy ordinances and the prophets profaned the Word of the Lord for their own ambition and purpose.

Prophets That Prophesy In Baal

"And I have seen folly in the prophets of Samaria; they prophesied in Baal, and caused my people Israel to err."

Jeremiah 23:13 (KJV)

Let me give you a brief summary of who Baal is. Baal was known as the fertility God in Middle Eastern communities. His name means, "owner" or "lord." During Israel's time in the land of Canaan Baal worship was an enemy to the exclusive worship of the true and living God. It was the primary reason for the destruction and exile of Israel and Judah (2 Kings

17:7-20; 21:10-15). Baal worship became idolatry for Israel; they broke the first commandment (Exodus 20:3-5).

Let me note one ritualistic practice of Baal worship. Adults would gather around the altar of Baal, as infants were burned alive as sacrificial offerings to the deity. The ritual was designed to produce economic prosperity by prompting Baal to bring rain. This was not just a form of abortion, but a spiritual sacrifice of the next generation.

So, it says, "I have seen folly, (frivolity, lack of seriousness, light-heartedness), in the prophets of Samaria; they **prophesied in Baal**, and caused my people Israel to err" (Jeremiah 23:13). Samaria was the city the ten tribes belonged to. They prophesied in Baal and from Baal.

Hearts full of idolatry will eventually prophesy God's people away from what's sacred, holy, and acceptable. They carry seduction in their mouths, saying all the right things but with the wrong spirit (Acts 16:16-19). In some cases, their words may come to pass, but the source is not from the Spirit of God.

"And I saw three unclean spirits coming out of the mouth of the dragon, the beast, and the false prophet."

Revelation 16:13 (KJV)

Satan has henchmen that do his work. "And why marvel, Satan himself is able to be transformed into an angel of light" (2 Corinthians 11:14). When prophets prophesy by Baal, they lead the Body of Christ away from God's heart, nature, and from presenting our bodies as living sacrifices (Romans 12:1-2). God's holiness and standard are literally mocked at. Flesh is promoted in the name of the Lord, all while unclean spirits are being released. The end result is that the spirit of err is embraced over the Spirit of Truth.

"I have seen also in the prophets of Jerusalem an horrible thing: they commit adultery, and walk in lies: they strengthen also the hands of evildoers, that none doth return from his wickedness; they are all of them unto me as Sodom, and the inhabitants thereof as Gomorrah."

Jeremiah 23:14 (KJV)

The prophets in Jerusalem didn't prophesy by Baal, but in the name of the true, living God. They were not as the prophets who prophesied by Baal, yet those prophets degraded and debauched themselves while prophesying in the name of God. Unrepented prophets are the most dangerous to the church. Prophets and prophetic people who preach fire and brimstone understand the message of sonship. They know apostolic and prophetic language, yet many have aborted the lifestyle that accompanies it (1 Corinthians 9:27).

The prophets in Samaria degraded God's people through idolatry but the prophets of Jerusalem through immoralities. Jeremiah said, "I have **seen** in the prophets of Jerusalem an **horrible** thing: they commit adultery and walk in lies" (Jeremiah 23:14). This does not mean that every prophet who has fallen into sin or been overtaken in a fault is typical of what I'm writing about, nevertheless, it is a problem within the Body of Christ that needs to be addressed.

There are those of whom I've seen do this **horrible** thing. They preach holiness but they live far from it themselves. They scream sonship but have never truly been a son. They know what needs to be said to try and throw people off their scent. Keep in mind, these were God's prophets but they had succumbed to immoral practices that were transferred to the nation of Israel.

Sexual impurity has overcome the church from the pulpit to the door. I personally believe that when the whole head is sick, won't repent, and get healed, it eventually affects the body. Kenneth Hagin Sr. once said, "what a pastor won't deal with in his congregation will eventually get in his pulpit." I will say, "what you won't deal with in your pulpit (ministers), will eventually get in your congregants." How can you really tell your congregants not to fornicate when you are as a leader? This is why Paul told Timothy to "be an example to the flock in purity" (1 Timothy 4:12).

The prophetic ministry has lost its purity because the vessels have lost their purity. We must purge out the old leaven of the prophetic and become a new lump. Many are preaching one thing but displaying another, and it's causing confusion. When the prophetic has been subdued by the spirit of Jezebel and people are seduced into sexual sins and spiritual idolatry, eating things sacrificed unto idols (Revelation 2:20).

Today, we live in a society when many prophets want to live as close to the world as they can, without departing from iniquity; all while using God's name (2 Timothy 2:19). Some choose to adopt the worldly appearances of our day while prophesying in the name of God. It's confusion! "A man shall not lie down with a beast; his sin nature (the world) (Leviticus 18:23). "Unclean spirits, like frogs came out of the mouth of the dragon, the **beast** and the false prophets." This is representative of Satan's trinity (Revelation 16:13).

Prophets, we must earnestly take time to examine ourselves and see if we are really aligned with the heart of God and with the Holy scriptures.

Purifying Our Motivation

"And seekest thou great things for thyself? seek them not: for, behold, I will bring evil upon all flesh, saith the LORD: but thy life will I give unto thee for a prey in all places whither thou goest."

In this hour, ungodly ambition has entered the hearts of many prophets and prophetic ministers. Ambition is good when it is harnessed with the right motivation. Ambition is defined as, "a strong desire to do or achieve something." Ambition, in and of itself, is not bad. It is only a problem when people desire and pursue success with impure motives. Motives matter to God; they reveal the true intent of the heart.

"²Ye lust, and have not: ye kill, and desire to have, and cannot obtain: ye fight and war, yet ye have not, because ye ask not. ³ Ye ask, and receive not, because ye ask amiss, that ye may consume it upon your lusts."

James 4:2-3 (KJV)

The ungodly ambition of many prophets has become their undoing. Ungodly ambition won't allow you to wait on your ministry. It causes you to break rank and rules which God, and godly leadership have set in place as parameters to help you grow properly. In this era of personal prophecy, when it comes to what God wants to do in an individual's life, many have jumped the gun after receiving a few prophecies; not realizing that their first anointing is always to serve.

David was prophesied to and anointed King at a young age, but he immediately went back to tending his father's sheep; being faithful over that which belonged to another man (Luke 16:12). Without the right fathering and mentorship, people often get off course pursuing their promise while despising the process. As a result, men and women start desiring a reputation rather than waiting on the season when they can no longer be hidden (Exodus 2:3; Luke 12:2).

"Jesus made Himself of no reputation but humbled Himself and became **obedient unto death;** even the death of the cross" (Philippians 2:8). Jesus died twice. His first death was of His will, in the garden of Gethsemane and His second death was His life, while on the cross (Philippians 2:8; Matthew 26:36-46).

I believe the Holy Spirit is purifying our hearts concerning our motivation in this season. God will take His time killing ungodly ambition in His prophets. This is why it takes a while before He raises up a prophet. You must pass the test of wrong ambition (motives) until all you want is His will and way in your life; then you are ready.

God's prophets can't be bought because they've already been purchased by God Himself. Their hearts have been purified by the refiner's fire and the dross has been taken away. Years ago, when I was a young prophet preaching in Virginia, I ran across some older prophets in a restaurant. They said they'd heard me on the radio and one of them tried to impress me with his material possessions. He began talking about his fancy sports cars and expensive shoes. Then he said he could help me get where I was trying to go. I think he assumed I was impressionable as a young man in ministry, but none of his material possessions moved me because God had already purified my motivation toward ministry. I had an Apostle and mentorship in my life which helped cultivate the right heart in me.

When you're seeking great things for yourself, you stop seeking the things that belong to Christ (Jeremiah 45:5). The Bible says, if you have no rule over your spirit, you're like a city without walls. Everything gets in you and everything goes out (Proverbs 28:25).

Fighting for A Pure Heart

"The heart is deceitful above all things, and desperately wicked: who can know it? "

Jeremiah 17:9 (KJV)

"Then Satan entered the heart of Judas Iscariot, who was one of the twelve apostles."

Luke 22:3 (CEV)

"Take heed unto thyself, and unto the doctrine; continue in them: for in doing this thou shalt both save thyself, and them that hear thee."

1 Timothy 4:16 (KJV)

"Guard your heart with all diligence; for out of it are the issues of life."

Proverbs 4:23 (KJV)

In order to maintain pure motivation and ambition, the heart has to be examined honestly. People can start out with the right heart, motivation, and ambition, but over time, good men and women can become bad. Solomon started out right, yet his heart was stolen by his many strange wives (I Kings 11:1-9). They turned him away from the true and living God. As a prophet, you must understand that the war is for your heart. Where your heart is, is where your treasure will be (Matthew 6:21). From the heart proceeds all manner of sin (Matthew 15:19).

David had a man killed and stole his wife. He later repented and said, "God create in me a clean heart and renew a right spirit within me" (2 Samuel 11-12; Psalm 51:10). Prophets must examine their hearts and motives daily.

Jeremiah said, "the heart is deceitful above all things and desperately wicked: who can know it" (Jeremiah 17:9)? None of us are as good as we think we are. The Bible says, "if any man think he stands, let him take heed lest he fall" (1 Corinthians 10:12). When deceit gets in the heart, if not careful, we become susceptible to a fall of some sort.

The Bible says, "David was a man after God's own heart," yet in one season his heart deceived him because lust entered it. His heart was hardened through the deceitfulness of sin.

Who can know the heart? Therefore, we should pay close attention to the subtleties of our hearts. Satan will work overtime to pervert the heart of a prophet, in an effort to turn him/her into one of his ministers (2 Corinthians 11:14-15). Satan tempts all genuine prophets to try and gain entrance into their hearts, sSo the prophet must be the first to know when lust, greed, wrong motivation, pride, etc. is trying to enter their heart. One must guard the heart, acknowledging and quickly repenting of error as soon as it is revealed by the Spirit. "Take heed unto thyself," is what Paul admonished Timothy to do (1 Timothy 4:16).

Avoid Craftiness

"But have renounced the hidden things of dishonesty, not walking in craftiness, nor handling the word of God deceitfully; but by manifestation of the truth commending ourselves to every man's conscience in the sight of God."

2 Corinthians 4:2 (KJV)

In order to purify the prophetic, we have to renounce our former practices in some areas. The word renounce in this passage of scripture means to, "disown." Paul is saying that as true ministers, we are to disown hidden things; the things that the natural eye can't see but the prophet knows are there. Hidden things; those things that are private, inward, and secret. Prophets must practice integrity when no one is looking. The dishonest things that no one else sees or hears must be renounced.

The dishonesty of a prophet can destroy his or her ministry. In this internet age, I've known prophets to get on individuals' social media pages and gather information, then supposedly give a word of knowledge to those individuals; as though they received it from God. There are some who will prophesy to an individual what they were told by another person. The list goes on, but in order to purify the prophetic, we need to renounce the secret, private, and inward dishonesty that lies within ourselves.

There is too much dishonesty and craftiness in our prophetic circles. Many handle the Word of God deceitfully; beguiling unstable souls, teaching things they ought not for filthy lucre sake (Titus 1:11). We must ask God to search us, and if there be any evil way in us, to lead us into righteousness (Psalm 139: 23-24). Unlike Balaam, we can't be satisfied with prophesying accurately while allowing our motivation to honor God to be so distant (Numbers 22-24).

✌ CHAPTER SEVEN ৯

"Ministering to the Lord"

"And the child Samuel ministered unto the LORD before Eli. And the word of the LORD was precious in those days; there was no open vision."

1 Samuel 3:1 (KJV)

"And she was a widow of about fourscore and four years, which departed not from the temple, but served God with fastings and prayers night and day."

Luke 2:37 (KJV)

"And it came to pass in those days, that he went out into a mountain to pray, and continued all night in prayer to God."

Luke 6:12 (KJV)

One thing I believe that's missing from the lives of ministers of the gospel; prophets in particular, is true intimacy with the Father. Many have neglected the discipline of ministering unto the Lord, which is every prophet's first ministry. We have put the cart before the horse. We have run after performance and neglected process. Many have titles; without being taught and many have not waited on their ministry. Many have honor with having experienced true humility (Proverbs 15:33).

Our ministries and the function of the prophetic office, should be birthed out of our relationship with Christ and the Holy Spirit. As a child, Samuel was trained by Eli and taught the necessity of ministering before the Lord. Eli taught him his priestly duties. Prophets don't just minister to people; they also minister unto the Lord.

A strong prophet will receive impartation from the life of Jesus by the working of the Holy Spirit, which allows them to minister a Jesus ministry in the Earth. They will operate in the fullness of the blessing of Jesus Christ (Romans 15:29). Jesus Himself, made it a habitual custom to withdraw from the multitudes for a time, to pray and spend time ministering before the Father. If a minister is to stay on the cutting edge of what God is doing, they must stay in constant fellowship with Him.

Prophets don't pray for material possessions, although that may be one of the benefits of a prayer life of one who is seeking first the Kingdom of God (Matthew 6:33). True prophets are lovers of the presence of God. They delight in seeking God for their ministry and live from their relationship with God (Amos 5:6). You can't give what you have not first received from God. It is through ministering unto the Lord that we receive from God by prayer, the Word, and worship. This is what makes us able ministers (2 Corinthians 3:6).

Prophets must spend more time with God than the environments in which they live. They must keep themselves unspotted from the world. The multitudes could be our undoing if we fail to withdraw frequently for our own personal time of ministry unto the Lord. We must stay in step with God and not the world we live in. We are to be in this world but not of it (John 15:19). Jesus was able to carry out the Father's will because He knew how to withdraw from the crowds and minister to God. Sowing in the spirit causes you to reap of the Spirit. You can't release God if you haven't been with God.

"Now when they saw the boldness of Peter and John, and perceived that they were unlearned and ignorant men, they marvelled; and they took knowledge of them, that they had been with Jesus."

Acts 4:13 (KJV)

Peter was the disciple who denied the Lord in one season, but on the day of Pentecost, he boldly proclaimed Him. Read Acts 2-4 at your leisure.

In chapter 4, Peter and John were brought before the Sanhedrin counsel for healing a man and preaching the resurrection of the dead through Jesus (Acts 3). There were two things their adversaries recognized.

1. They saw their boldness.
2. They acknowledged they were unlearned men who had been with Jesus.

Ministering to the Lord produces undeniable fruit that even your adversaries cannot deny. A leader who lives in the presence of God will come out of the mount with a shine (glory) on his or her face (Exodus 34:29-35). It will affect every part of their life.

There are many who say they pray and seek God but, when they come out of their prayer closet their speech betrays them. Too many prophets/prophetesses say they are having 5am morning glory and 24-hour prayer meetings, but flesh is still being promoted in many areas of their lives and ministries.

We should be the first partakers of being in God's presence. Remember, Jesus was transfigured on the mountain of transfiguration (Matthew 17:1-2). We should declare, like Peter, "it's good for us to be here." Ministering before the Lord should affect us from the inside out. Peter and John had a boldness that was birthed from intimacy. They were undaunted by their position or status. God made their faces like a rock before their adversaries.

We don't need any more prophets who have a form of godliness, but who deny the power thereof (2 Timothy 3:5). We need those who have allowed their fellowship with Christ to produce His nature and ministry within them. Men should be able to boldly say, "we can't deny they've been with Him." They may not like you or your style, but they won't be able to deny you've been with Jesus!

If we are really going to make an impact in our world, it must become evident that we've been with Jesus.

Serving the Lord with Fastings and Prayers Night and Day (Luke 2:37)

The Bible recognizes Anna, a prophetess who served God with fastings and prayers. Strong's Dictionary #3000, defines the word "served" as "latreuo: lat-ryoo-o" in the Greek. It is from the root word latris and means, "a hired menial, to minister (to God), to render religious homage-serve, do the service, worship." I believe we will begin to see an authentic release of Jesus' ministry on the Earth again, when we embrace the ministry of serving God in fastings and prayers.

Many ministers of our day lack spiritual discipline on so many levels. The prophetess Anna shows us a different kind of ministry, which is to the Lord and not to man. No doubt, she probably taught the women of Israel and declared the mind of God prophetically. The Bible tells us she served God with fastings and prayers. What a great compliment to a prophetess of the Lord!

Her strength was her discipline to live in the temple without the name and popularity other prophets had. She was content with a ministry unto the Lord. Most prophets/prophetesses don't know the power and honor it is to serve God with fastings and prayers. The power of the prophet/prophetess comes from their discipline. Fasting humbles the soul and makes us more sensitive to spiritual things. It causes the flesh and soulish realm to give way to the Spirit.

"Though this outward man perishes, yet my inward man is renewed day by day."

2 Corinthians 4:16

Fasting is buffering the body to bring it under subjection (1 Corinthians 9:27). As prophets minister to the Lord through fasting, it helps them remain God's prophet and not give way to sensuality. Praying builds the prophets' spirit up. He or she establishes a channel whereby the Holy Spirit can communicate spiritual language and thoughts, through the ministry of prayer. It was through prayer that Jesus manifested the life and thoughts of His Father. Prayer and fellowship with His Father were the strength of Jesus' life and ministry.

When prophets serve God with prayers, their revelation of scripture and their prophetic accuracy increases. Many have stepped out into their ministries without the discipline of prayer as their foundation. As a result, many faint in the day of adversity (Proverbs 24:10). There is no real presence on these individuals. They are like clouds and winds with no rain in them (Proverbs 25:14).

When a prophet forfeits prayer for long periods, they become stale in the anointing. They become redundant and prophetically obsolete. I've learned that God doesn't send prophets who don't have a prayer life. All prophets should be intercessors first. Abraham was, Moses was, the list goes on and on. Although prayer is a spiritual discipline, intercession is a way of life for true prophets; one must cultivate it.

When rebuking the prophets of his day, Jeremiah said, "I have not sent these prophets, yet they ran: I have not spoken to them, yet they prophesied" (Jeremiah 23:21). In today's society, everyone wants to claim the title, "prophet." Nine out of every ten people believe they are prophets, yet most have never sat under a senior leader for any length of time to wait on their ministry.

Like Ahimaaz, many have a zeal without a message. Many want to run without the tidings of the Lord. (2 Samuel 18:19-20). Ahimaaz went to David's captain (senior leader) and said, "let me run." Joab told him, "thou shalt not bear tidings this day but **another day**." Seasoned leaders know when you are ready. Joab sent Cushi, a more seasoned man who had wisdom and experience, but Ahimaaz kept pushing the issue instead of waiting on his ministry. Joab finally granted him his desire. Read this at your leisure. You will see that Ahimaaz got to David with the tidings (news) about the outcome of the battle and of his son Absalom, first. However, we find that when David asked him of Absalom, he didn't have the grace or the wisdom to articulate it. He ran, but he had nothing to say when he got there. He was a messenger but he was without the Lord's message. Read 2 Samuel 18 in detail.

Jeremiah told the people of Judah, God said, "if they would have **stood** in my **counsel**, and caused my people to hear my words, then they should have turned from their evil way and from the evil of their doings" (Jeremiah 23:22). Prophets must stand in God's **counsel**. The Hebrew word for counsel is "**cowd, sode**" (Strong's Concordance #H5475). It means: "a session, company of persons, by implication, intimacy, a secret assembly." True prophets carry the secrets of God because they live in His counsel. True prophets commune with the Holy Spirit; He is their consultant for the Kingdom of God and for the Lord's people. They cause people to hear God's Words.

In contrast, false prophets speak smooth words and convey messages that cause people to deviate from God's Word. They cater to itching ears, giving people what they want to hear rather than what they need to hear (2 Timothy 4:3).

The children of Israel didn't want to hear God speak lest they die (Exodus 20:19). When true prophets speak, it kills the flesh and worldly desires out of believers. This is why most churches have an ought with God's true prophets. Mainstream Christianity doesn't have many platforms for true prophets.

❧ CHAPTER EIGHT ❧

"Prophets Must Learn How to Keep A Poor Spirit"

In the sermon on the mount, Jesus shared what is referred to as the Beatitudes, or kingdom attitudes. These are inward kingdom character traits every believer should pursue. As we are discussing the prophetic ministry, God has shown me that prophets need to give more attention to their kingdom attitudes. In this chapter, we will discuss the importance of being "poor in spirit."

Let me begin by defining what it means to be poor in spirit. First of all, being poor in spirit has nothing to do with money or a lack thereof. In this passage of scripture Jesus was teaching about the inner state of a believer's heart and spirit. I've seen prophets lose their cutting edge because they didn't keep a poor spirit.

According to Strong's Dictionary #64434, poor in spirit means: "to crouch; a beggar." It signifies a need or an awareness of humility. In a spiritual sense "poor in spirit" speaks of the following:

1. Humility

2. Dependency

3. Staying hungry

4. Staying teachable.

As we take a moment to discuss these in detail please be mindful that this list is by no means exhaustive.

Humility

Prophets with poor spirits understand the power of humility. When a prophet operates in a poor spirit, he or she opens their life up for a greater measure of grace. "But he giveth more grace. Wherefore he saith he resists the proud and gives grace to the humble" (James 4:6). To have a poor spirit is to walk in humility.

When a prophet becomes prideful, they lose their edge and stifle their anointing. Having a poor spirit is to rid oneself of pride and vain glory. It is humbling oneself under the mighty hand of God. Jesus' ministry flowed from a poor spirit. He finished His purpose because He never lost a poor spirit. Consider these scriptures:

"⁵Let this mind be in you, which was also in Christ Jesus, ⁶Who being in the form of God, thought it not robbery to be equal with God: ⁷But made himself of no reputation, and took upon him the form of a servant, and was made in the likeness of men: ⁸And being found in fashion of a man he humbled himself, and became obedient unto death, even the death of the cross. ⁹Wherefore God has highly exalted him, and given him a name which is above every name"

Philippians 2:5-9 (KJV)

A poor spirit is a mindset that prophets must possess to remain obedient to God. This mind must be in the prophet so that he or she can always be useful when needed. No assignment is too small or too big. The poor in spirit are willing to lose their reputation for the advancement of the Kingdom. A humble spirit gets low so Christ can be seen. We decrease so He can increase (John 3:30). We willfully take the lowest seat in the room for our master. Our posture is broken before God and those we are called to serve.

Pride on a prophet/prophetess causes the apothecary to send forth a stinking savor (Ecclesiastes 10:1). It puts a bad smell in the prophet's anointing. Like the tax collector, it causes us to stand afar off beating our breast. The humble prophet doesn't try to justify him/herself. They'd rather allow Christ to justify them and bring validity to their ministry (Luke 18:13-14).

Stay Little In Your Own Eyes

"And Samuel said, when thou wast little in thine own sight, wast thou not made the head of the tribes of Israel, and the LORD anointed thee king over Israel?"

1 Samuel 15:17 (KJV)

Having a poor spirit means, I see it but I don't know it. Saul was anointed the first king over Israel. He disobeyed God and was rejected because of it. Samuel rebuked Saul for his disobedience with these words: "When thou wast little in thine own sight..." Prophets have to learn to not see their greatness. To be poor in the spirit is to be small in your own eyes. This keeps grace flowing in your life and helps fuel your pursuit for more of God's presence.

Throughout the years, I've had people say many wonderful things about my ministry, yet I've seen none of it. That's what has kept me hungry for God and poor in spirit. When you can see how gifted and anointed you are, you are headed for disaster on so many levels. I'm often asked, "how do you get the revelation you walk in?" To me it's simple. . . I stay small in my own eyes. Don't allow the praises of men to open your eyes. Stay a Gideon as long as you can, and God will do great things with you (Judges 6). Always see your need for more of God. Never let your gift or anointing take the place of God and your relationship with the Holy Spirit.

Dependency on God

"**7 But what things were gain to me, those I counted loss for Christ. 8 Yea doubtless, and I count all things but loss for the excellency of the knowledge of Christ Jesus my Lord: for whom I have suffered the loss of all things, and do count them but dung, that I may win Christ.**"

Philippians 3:7-8 (KJV)

"And he humbled thee, and suffered thee to hunger, and fed thee with manna, which thou knewest not, neither did thy fathers know; that he might make thee know that man doth not live by bread only, but by every word that proceedeth out of the mouth of the Lord doth man live."

Deuteronomy 8:2 (KJV)

Those who are poor in spirit have a dependency on God. Prophets can never lose their dependency upon God. Our strength can never come from us. A person who is poor spirit acknowledges their need for God.

The prophet who is poor in spirit remembers all the ways the Lord has taken him/her in their process of becoming a mature prophet. They never lose sight of the seasons of humility and testing they've had to endure. Like Jacob, their limp is a constant reminder that they wrestled with God to become who they are and that it cost them (Genesis 32:24-31). We consider ourselves in everything we say and do (Galatians 6:1).

Humility teaches us how to talk and how to order our words. Those who are poor in spirit long to be in God's presence and depend on God to supply their spiritual needs. When we stop depending on God for His grace, ability, and endowment, we become prideful and our ministries start lacking authentic presence. As prophets, we lose our edge doing ministry without God (Mark 16).

Jesus continually depended on the Father to endow Him with revelation, guidance, strength, and courage for His assignment; He remained poor in spirit. Paul knew that in order to have more of God, he had to lose himself. He shows this in Philippians 3:4-8, when he began talking about his credentials and his accomplishments, as an Israelite who could no doubt trust in the flesh. He understood that if he wanted to know Jesus in a more excellent way, he had to depend upon the Holy Spirit and not in his own flesh.

Paul said, "But what things were gain to me, those I counted loss for Christ" (Philippians 1:37). Prophets must always keep their liabilities in sight. Liabilities are those things that prevent you from being dependent upon God. One must learn how to count things as loss for Christ. That could consist of your reputation, a relationship, a job, or an accomplishment. The secret to getting more of God is counting things as dung. Doing so says, "I don't trust in horses or chariots, but in the name of the Lord" (Psalm 20:7)!

Stay Hungry

The poor in spirit learn how to stay hungry. Prophets who stay hungry bring forth fruit in every season (Psalm 1:3). To stay hungry for the things of God for a long period is to be poor in spirit. The Bible says, "they that hunger and thirst after righteousness shall be filled" (Matthew 5:6). Prophets who stay hungry, stay relevant. They go from faith to faith, glory to glory, and from strength to strength (Romans 1:17; 2 Corinthians 3:16-18; Psalm 84:7). God continuously fills them with Word, righteousness, and revelation. Their barns (spirits) are filled with plenty of God (Proverbs 3:10). David said, "as the deer pants after the water brooks, so panteth my soul after thee, O God" (Psalm 42:1).

Prophets, never lose your pant (longing) for God. To hunger and thirst after righteousness is to be poor in spirit. Men will praise you and tell you how wonderful you are, and God may use you in a mighty way, but never get drunk off your own wine (success). That will be the day you lose your hunger (Genesis 9:21).

The poor in spirit know how to stay empty, even when they are full. "A person who is full tramples on a honeycomb, but to a hungry person, any bitter thing is sweet" (Proverbs 27:7 CSB). Prophets should continually empty themselves of vain glory and always be ready to receive more of God; being conversant with God, like Enoch, until we are no longer (Genesis 5:24). If we truly desire more of God's glory and nature, our walk with Him should be consistent and fresh.

"He hath <u>filled</u> the hungry with <u>good things</u>; and the <u>rich</u> he hath sent <u>empty</u> away."

Luke 1:53 (KJV)

Mary's prophetic song is called the "Magnificat." She sings, "He has filled the hungry with good things; and the rich he hath sent empty (vain) away." Hungry people get filled with good things. If you're too rich, you get sent away empty according to Mary's song. The Laodicean church is a great example of this.

"17 Because thou sayest, I am rich, and increased with goods, and have need of nothing; and knowest not that thou art wretched, and miserable, and poor, and blind, and naked: 18 I counsel thee to buy of me gold tried in the fire, that thou mayest be rich; and white raiment, that thou mayest be clothed, and that the shame of thy nakedness do not appear; and anoint thine eyes with eye salve, that thou mayest see."

Revelation 3:17-18 (KJV)

The Laodicean church was rebuked by Jesus for being lukewarm. They saw themselves in the wrong light. They said they were rich, increased with goods, and in need of nothing. They had blind spots and couldn't see them. They were rich but not toward God (Luke 12:21). This sounds like most of our churches here in America. They think more highly of themselves than they ought. Many are trying to pass off gain as godliness, which is an error (1 Timothy 6:6). Jesus said they were, "poor, blind, and naked." In essence, they have lost the poor spirit they once had.

True wealth is found in Christ and in His graces. God has blessed many of His servants with fame, favor, and wealth; for His glory. Unfortunately, many of them have lost the poor spirit they once had. Their success has robbed them of their hunger. They have stuff but they are no longer truly blessed by God because the Bible says, "blessed are the poor in spirit, for theirs is the kingdom of Heaven" (Matthew 5:3).

To remedy the problem with the Laodicean church, Jesus told them, "come buy of me gold tried in the fire; and thou mayest be rich. . ." In other words, Jesus was saying, "fall back in love with Me and do things my way. Put your life back under my Lordship again."

Prophets, I counsel you to develop a poor spirit again; get your hunger back. Perhaps you keep leaving God's presence empty because you're too full of your day, your cares, or your sin.

Stay Teachable

"Teach me thy way, O LORD; I will walk in thy truth: unite my heart to fear thy name."

Psalm 86:11 (KJV)

"Give instruction to a wise man, and he will be yet wiser: teach a just man, and he will increase in learning."

Proverbs 9:9 (KJV)

Sometimes remaining teachable is easier said than done, especially as a gifted prophet. Giftedness is an enemy to a poor spirit.

Over the years, I have personally found that remaining teachable and accountable, through covenant relationships with senior leaders, fathering Apostles, and prophets, has kept me poor in spirit. No one man knows everything nor has all the answers. We are called the "Body of Christ" and every joint supplies to bring about increase (Ephesians 4:16).

I've seen prophets and prophetic people self-destruct because they became unteachable. When this happens, one forfeits growth and maturity. Spiritual pride settles in and one wants to be the greatest among us. One fails to realize that even a pitcher needs someone or something to pour into it. If you're the smartest in the room, find another room. You'll never be at your best alone, this is why the Bible says, "two are better than one, for if the one fall, the other can help him up" (Ecclesiastes 4:9-12). Jesus sent His disciples out two-by-two.

Those who are poor in spirit understand that their growth is connected to a person as well as to God. When you pray, "Lord teach me your way," God will begin putting people in your life, both directly and indirectly, to help teach and train you. It may be through books, cd's, or through personal relationships. Can you imagine how arrogant we would be if we learned everything from God Himself? The Bible says, we are partakers of the gifts and talents the Holy Spirit has given each of us (1 Peter 4:10-11).

Those who are poor in spirit are always increasing in their knowledge and adding to their faith daily. The

Lord's prophets will remain blessed and full of substance if they would live by this principle.

Every Elisabeth needs a Mary from time to time. Revelation is always multiplied when I'm in the company of other prophets. When prophets minister together as a team, they minister with a greater level of revelation and accuracy.

"As the new wine is found in the cluster, and one saith, Destroy it not; for a blessing is in it: so will I do for my servants' sakes, that I may not destroy them all."

(Isaiah 65:8)

Newness is always found in the <u>cluster</u>; not just one.

❧ CHAPTER NINE ❧

"Prophetic Protocol"

One of the elements of prophetic ministry that doesn't get enough attention is the area of prophetic protocol. This refers to the do's and don'ts of prophetic ministry. In this chapter, I will provide you with a list of helpful protocols for prophets and prophetic ministers. Please note: this list is by no means exhaustive.

I will begin with an explanation of the term, "in house prophets." In house prophets are those prophets who serve and are committed to a local church or ministry.

When it comes to prophetic protocol here are specific points that will help ensure you are operating effectively and in the order of God.

1. Submit your spirit to the set man or woman of God.

2. Submit your gift to the local Pastor.

3. Pray for your leaders every day.

4. Never get caught in church cliques.

- They will hinder prophetic discernment and accuracy.

5. Show up to corporate prayer.

- It helps leaders trust your ability to release pure streams.
- It shows humility and that you're not above corporate fellowship.
- It can yield opportunity for your gift to be used and bring encouragement to others who are in attendance.

6. Never rebuke your senior leadership openly.

- Mature prophets are trusted by their leadership.
- You should have the ability to hold the word in until you can have a meeting with your senior leader(s).

7. Never prophesy the complaints of the people who have come to you with their concerns about the

leadership, the ministry, or as a result of a decision that has been made.

8. Your prophecies should bring direction to a local assembly; not confusion.

9. Your prophecies shouldn't make congregants doubt their leadership.

10. Your prophecies should stir people in the direction of supporting the vision.

11. When prophesying a warning or correction in a local ministry, it must be done with wisdom and love; without losing the authority of the prophetic message.

12. Young prophets, prophetesses, and prophetic ministers should attend all Schools of the Prophets offered in their local church.

- This gives the opportunity to learn and gain experience, while observing the senior prophet or teacher in action.
- It helps you develop your own prophetics (prophetic flow).

13. Prophets should enforce what their leader(s) have been teaching and preaching.

14. Prophets should be watchmen in their local church.

- They should see what's approaching the ministry, whether it be good or bad.
- They should see in the heavenly realm and receive guidance and direction for the ministry.

15. Prophets should show the most courage when warfare hits a local church.

Itinerant Prophets

1. Stay connected to a local pastor and church.

- When you come off the road, you need to be poured into.

2. Don't substitute ministry for a vibrant relationship with Jesus, the Holy Spirit, and the Word of God.

3. Preaching the same message too many times will cause God to wring that message out to dry.

- Don't be lazy. Take the time to seek God for fresh revelation.

- Every ministry doesn't need your favorite top 10 messages.

4. Never ask to preach at another man's ministry, if you're not sought out.
- Having a great relationship with someone may be an exception to the rule.

5. Don't try to be so knowledgeable in your delivery that you forget to minister to your audience.
- Don't lose God's message trying to show people how knowledgeable you are.

6. If you are called upon to do a revival at a local church, don't try to do everything in one night.
- Don't wear the people out with long services.
- When the anointing has lifted, it's time for the minster to take his or her seat.

7. When invited to a church, walk in humility while you are there.

8. Never take phone numbers from congregants without the pastors' consent.

9. Always counsel congregants of a local church to support their local pastor.

- Don't get caught in the middle of something you don't fully understand.
- An exception to this rule is if a pastor is not living according to the Word of God, and the people are being deceived, or led into captivity by his or her actions.

10. When rebuking or correcting in a local church, always seek God on how to deliver the message in wisdom.

- The ultimate goal is for the congregants to receive it for their edification and not their destruction.

11. Don't try to seek out good givers at meetings you are invited to.

- Don't try to crab supporters from another man's ministry for personal gain.

12. When traveling with an assistant, don't assume every church can afford them in their budget. They called for you!

13. Never go to a ministry without the intent of blessing that ministry.

14. Don't carry what you heard about another leader or ministry in your spirit.

15. Single men and women: As guest speakers, don't lust after and pursue other singles within a local church.

- No one should know where you are lodging while you are there as a guest.

16. Married men and women should make mention of their spouses while on the road.

When Prophesying

1. When prophesying, don't ramble. That's not prophesying.

2. Ask few questions when giving personal prophecies.

3. It is not wise to give twenty-minute prophecies to one person.

4. Don't try to prophesy to everyone in the room on the first night of the meeting.

5. Stay in your grace when prophesying.

- Don't try to flow like other prophets.

6. Don't be over dramatic when prophesying.

7. Avoid prophesying to people you have prior information about, especially if there is tension between the two of you. Doing so will led to greater problems (tension).

8. Discern the timing of certain prophecies.

- Just because you saw or heard it, doesn't mean you need to release it.

9. Get the wisdom of Nathan when prophesying sin issues to leaders. This also applies when ministering sensitive things in public.

10. Some prophecies aren't for everybody to hear.

- Know when to speak in the ear.

11. Don't point your finger in anyone's face when prophesying.

- Don't be aggressive when delivering prophetic messages.

12. Keep your breath fresh while prophesying.

13. Avoid prophesying during offering time. Sometimes this is not possible, but it is a good rule to live by as a prophetic minister.
- We shouldn't want people being motivated to give because of prophecy.

14. Don't let people turn you into a psychic just because they need or want a word.

15. Don't let reward or money be the motivation for you prophesying.

16. Stay away from prophesying people into marriages. There are some exceptions to this rule.

17. Your prophecies should lead people to Christ, not to you.

18. Your prophecies should be rooted in the Word of God.

www.ingramcontent.com/pod-product-compliance
Lightning Source LLC
Chambersburg PA
CBHW072157090426
42740CB00012B/2300